HURRICANE HARVEY'S AFTERMATH

Hurricane Harvey's Aftermath

Place, Race, and Inequality in Disaster Recovery

Kevin M. Fitzpatrick and Matthew L. Spialek

NEW YORK UNIVERSITY PRESS
New York

NEW YORK UNIVERSITY PRESS
New York
www.nyupress.org

© 2020 by New York University
All rights reserved

References to Internet websites (URLs) were accurate at the time of writing. Neither the author nor New York University Press is responsible for URLs that may have expired or changed since the manuscript was prepared.

Library of Congress Cataloging-in-Publication Data
Names: Fitzpatrick, Kevin M., author. | Spialek, Matthew L., author.
Title: Hurricane Harvey's aftermath : place, race, and inequality in disaster recovery / Kevin M. Fitzpatrick and Matthew L. Spialek.
Description: New York : New York University Press, [2020] | Includes bibliographical references and index.
Identifiers: LCCN 2019041707 | ISBN 9781479800735 (cloth) | ISBN 9781479800759 (paperback) | ISBN 9781479800773 (ebook) | ISBN 9781479800780 (ebook)
Subjects: LCSH: Hurricane Harvey, 2017. | Hurricanes—Texas. | Hurricane damage—Texas. | Disaster relief—Texas.
Classification: LCC QC945 .F547 2020 | DDC 363.34/92209764—dc23
LC record available at https://lccn.loc.gov/2019041707

New York University Press books are printed on acid-free paper, and their binding materials are chosen for strength and durability. We strive to use environmentally responsible suppliers and materials to the greatest extent possible in publishing our books.

Manufactured in the United States of America

10 9 8 7 6 5 4 3 2 1

Also available as an ebook

To my family and most importantly my wife, Mary, who continues to support me and encourage my work. To all of the families who lost loved ones during Hurricane Harvey and are still working to put the pieces of their lives back together again.

—Kevin M. Fitzpatrick

To my parents, Larry and Diane Spialek. To all the survivors who shared their stories with us as they continue to heal after Harvey.

—Matthew L. Spialek

CONTENTS

List of Figures and Tables — ix

Preface — xi

1. A Hard Rain's A-Gonna Fall — 1

2. Who We Are — 26

3. Every Picture Tells a Story — 47

4. Anticipation — 70

5. Who'll Stop the Rain? — 92

6. After the Storm — 115

7. Changes — 140

Acknowledgments — 167

Notes — 169

References — 175

Index — 185

About the Authors — 189

LIST OF FIGURES AND TABLES

Table 2.1 Sociodemographics of Selected Counties for Interviewee Targets — 32

Figure 3.1 Apartment Cleanup — 49

Figure 3.2 Muddied Bicycle — 50

Figure 3.3 Houston Community College Warehouse Shelter — 52

Figure 3.4 Disaster Assistance (FEMA) Applications for Texas Counties — 57

Figure 3.5 House Stripped to the Studs — 58

Figure 3.6a–b Pearland Homes — 59

Figure 3.7a–b Corpus Christi Neighborhood — 61

Figure 3.8 DeWolfe's Four Phases of Disaster — 62

Figure 3.9 Volunteer Staging — 64

Figure 3.10 High Water Rescue — 65

Table 3.1 Displacement Outcomes — 51

Table 3.2 Satisfaction with Displacement Outcomes — 51

Table 3.3 How Much Disruption? — 54

Table 3.4 Percent Displacement Path by Race and Ethnicity   55

Table 3.5 Percent Reporting Damage by Race and Ethnicity   55

Table 3.6 Percent Satisfied with Government Response   69

Figure 4.1 Inclusion in the Community Self Scale   76

PREFACE

This book aims to tell a story of heartache, destruction, resilience, recovery, and hope. Funded by the National Science Foundation (NSF), a team of interviewers was deployed along the Texas Gulf Coast from Corpus Christi to Galveston to interview Hurricane Harvey survivors and record their stories. The goal of the project was to carefully uncover the stories behind resilience, response, and recovery, focusing on how different response and recovery looks for persons depending on who they are and where they live.

With over three hundred interviews, the complex data-gathering strategy attempted to carefully represent all impacted locations. We also selected individuals who relocated into shelters, hotels, and other alternative displacement locations in order to assess the long and difficult roads of disaster recovery. We know that some respondents have since moved back to their old neighborhoods, and others never had to leave. Some survivors have been working on their return home for more than two years, and others will likely never return. These survivors' stories are different, their circumstances are different, and the recovery process they are still experiencing is different too. Some of that difference is determined by who the survivors are. Like others telling this story before us,[1] we know that race, age, ethnicity, and socioeconomic status intersect in critical ways to either enhance or impede the response and recovery process. Related to this intersection of social and demographic factors is the role geographic location plays in the experience of disasters and the recovery process that follows. Like so much work that has been place-focused,[2] zip code continues to be an important determinant of a wide range of health and well-being outcomes. Disaster response and recovery appears to be no different.

We believe this is an important story to tell because it attempts to not only document individual recovery, but also to showcase how community resilience factors into the response and recovery equation. Just like individuals, some communities have been broken and will experience great pain and suffering in recovery compared to more resilient communities who will rebuild even stronger than before Hurricane Harvey hit. The power of place for everyday experiences and behavior is undeniable. Place is a key element in our identity and life experiences—a life whose quality, in turn, can be dramatically impacted by natural disasters. This is not just a story about Houston, Galveston, or Corpus Christi. It is also a story about the other lesser-known towns, such as Port Aransas, Pearland, Pasadena, Moss Hill, and Newton. Some of these towns had no idea what was coming, while others were prepared and ready to bear the full brunt of the storm. These different community stories, interwoven among the individual stories, are as complicated and diverse as the residents who lived in these places when Hurricane Harvey made landfall. Our hope is to provide a brief glimpse of these varied experiences in an effort to better understand the processes and why they need to change moving forward as our country prepares for the next big natural disaster along the coast.

1

A Hard Rain's A-Gonna Fall

Few people in the United States paid attention to the weather off the coast of Africa in August 2017. Every year, in that part of the world, hundreds of tropical waves and depressions come and go, and no one really remembers much about them. But one of those tropical depressions was different. In the early days of the month it began to take shape, and soon it would become a household name. As this yet-to-be-named tropical depression blew into the Caribbean, meteorologists took note as they typically do, modeling the probabilities of this storm becoming something significant. It wasn't until the storm entered the warm waters of the Gulf of Mexico that it intensified, gaining enormous strength as it churned its way toward the Texas coastline. Meteorologists eventually named this storm Harvey. People started paying attention, and they would never forget that name.

It seemed the rain would never stop. Harvey was definitely not shaping up to be your typical hurricane. By the time the storm made landfall four miles east of Rockport, Texas, on August 25, the ground was saturated, rivers overflowed their banks, and every major dam, levee, reservoir, creek, and bayou had either been compromised or exceeded its flood stage. Harvey became something to contend with: a Category 4 storm packing winds in excess of 130 miles per hour. Rainband after rainband pummeled towns up and down the coast, producing a historical rain the likes of which no one had witnessed in this part of the country. Harvey wound up generating the single greatest amount of rainfall in the history of the continental United States, breaking one record after another.[1]

For some cities, this much water might have been a major inconvenience, but for cities like Houston, Port Aransas, Corpus Christi, and Port Arthur, it amounted to an epic disaster because the water had no place to go but up. Just how much water was dumped on the coast during the storm? Officials estimate somewhere between 30 and 35 trillion gallons of water fell on cities along the coastal regions of Texas and Louisiana—enough water to fill the Chesapeake Bay, put an end to the California drought twice, or cover the entire state of Arizona with one foot of water.[2] It is hard to fathom that much water in one place, but that is exactly what the residents of Texas Gulf Coast communities had to do as the floodwaters rose.

At some point prior to the evening of August 25, and in the five or six days that followed, Texas Gulf Coast residents realized that the sandbags they'd filled and stacked in the days leading up to this storm were probably not going to make much of a difference this time. Most of the efforts to prevent the flooding of homes or businesses appeared to be futile. Could anyone have prepared for this much rain?

Many residents made the early decision to evacuate before Harvey made landfall—securing their homes as best they could; gathering their valuables, pets, and pictures; and leaving. For them, displacement meant contacting family in other parts of Texas or elsewhere and making plans to get out of the storm's path until things returned to "normal." Others made the decision to stay put, batten down the hatches, ride out the storm, and do whatever needed to be done in order to save their homes and belongings. Thousands of people had no choice when it came to evacuation. Without family or friends to turn to, or with little or no money to help with transport out of town or to pay for hotels, staying behind became the only option. That choice—or lack of choice—proved fatal for some. Many who did not evacuate would eventually find their way to public shelters. They might have been reluctant to go, but they were thankful to have somewhere to stay amid the hundred-year storm.

The American Red Cross opened shelters, the Federal Emergency Management Agency (FEMA) was mobilized, Salvation Army disaster teams were deployed, and a complicated set of partnerships was forged out of necessity to temporarily house thousands of people in the weeks and months after the storm. These shelters seemed to open up overnight, and people showed up, signed in, and sat on cots, on the floor, or wherever they could find a quiet place to rest. The people of Houston and the Texas Gulf Coast just waited, waited, and waited some more, wondering what would happen next.

Tent cities, warehouse towns, and shelter villages dotted the urban and rural landscape as a long, complicated process of waiting and recovery began. This process, like many before it, was fraught with poor planning, indecision, strained infrastructures, and a bureaucratic decision-making system that responded slowly to the complicated needs of the storm survivors—people who soon saw and felt how unequal the efforts of disaster rescue and recovery actually were.

Many residents had to be rescued from the rising floodwaters, which became an important part of Hurricane Harvey's survivor stories. We knew these stories would be as diverse as the impacted population, just as we expected the patterns of displacement to be vastly different depending upon the places from which the survivors had been displaced. Over ninety people died in Texas during Hurricane Harvey and its aftermath. Most drowned. Those who lost their lives were mothers, sons, daughters, husbands, wives, fathers, coaches, police officers, and teachers. Thousands of others were more fortunate. Some climbed to the second floor of their home or the roof of their apartment complex and waited until the floodwaters receded. Others waited days to be rescued. Some were lucky enough to find a pathway out of their neighborhood and be picked up by one of hundreds of rescue boats, including those from the "Cajun Navy" that descended on communities all along the coastal towns and cities of Texas and Louisiana. This group of ordinary citizens from Louisiana got together and decided to pack up their airboats and bass-fishing boats and make their way to Texas to help those in need. These volunteers made a difference, and we heard plenty of stories about similar people who just rolled up their sleeves and jumped in to help wherever they were needed.

This was not the first group of volunteers to show up at a natural disaster without the prompting of emergency management officials, government agencies, or disaster relief organizations. Such unsung heroes often appear amid disasters—"friendly responders" who assist communities where disaster rescue and recovery is too overwhelmed with calls and requests. During Harvey, people could not count on their calls for help being answered. Even the 911 calls were triaged in a way that some neighborhoods and locations got so backed up with requests that three or four days passed before first responders could arrive to help.

One thing was for certain in August 2017: recovery would not be simple. No one had a magic wand to wave that would speed up the process or ease the pain and suffering that comes with death, displacement, and destruction. Everyone's story was the same, yet everyone's story was different. The wide chasms separating the stories were, in part, driven by the complicated social intersections of race, place, and poverty. Particular nuances emerged depending on whether people rode out the storm or evacuated, whether people went to a hotel or a temporary shelter, and whether people lived in the urban or suburban areas or in the middle of nowhere. What continued to be an important part of the displacement and recovery narrative ever since Katrina was recognizing that the story and its ending would be dramatically different because of the neighborhood a person lived in when the storm hit, and whether that person was rich or poor, black or white, immobile or mobile, young or old.

Several very long weeks after the storm hit, it became apparent to us as researchers that geographic location was important in determining how people responded, recovered, and returned to their neighborhoods. The physical space people occupied mattered—the complicated social fabric knitting them together and characterizing the places they called home, and the level of preparedness or resilience in those places that was critical to that social fabric. The storm devastated certain neighborhoods, and sometimes the resilience cracked. Nevertheless, the indelible human spirit shone through, and people continued to help each other. Recovery began, and even though some communities were eventually abandoned, others began the long and difficult process of rebuilding.

An Emerging Story

We were committed to telling a story that needed to be told, as quickly as possible. Hurricane Harvey was one of several "billion dollar disasters" that took place during summer and early fall 2017. By the time Hurricane Maria made landfall in Puerto Rico in September, the news media and storytellers had packed up, left the Texas Gulf Coast, and headed elsewhere to begin telling a different story—leaving the people of Houston, Galveston, Beaumont, and Port Arthur behind, still traumatized and struggling with waning support from the vast network of disaster response and recovery organizations. The Red Cross quickly closed all of their shelters. The housing options became narrow and confining, plagued with uncertain futures. We believe this to be an important part of the Hurricane Harvey story, that Texas was left to figure things out when support moved on to meet the needs of other parts of the world facing disaster and devastation. The unprecedented impact of multiple natural disasters in a relatively short period of time in the United States and its territory of Puerto Rico has become an essential part of understanding the Texas Gulf Coast story.

The scope and magnitude of Maria's destruction, coupled with the public sparring between the White House and Puerto Rican officials, left the country to assume that Harvey response and recovery was going smoothly. Yet after months of listening to survivors tell their stories, we recognized that the Harvey "success story" (by the most charitable of estimates) was only partially true. The myth overshadowed the true narratives of individuals. We wanted to make sure those stories were told, while keeping critical eyes on the process of recovery from both human and social capital perspectives.

Months after the storm hit, stories continued to be recorded about Texas Gulf Coast communities where schools struggled to stay open and people still lived in RVs in their backyards. Recovery had slowed to a turtle's pace. Many residents were still waiting for support, materials, and restitution; yet despite the trauma, pain, and uncertainty, communities continued to work together to try to cope and recover.

One story circulated about Refugio, Texas, a small town forty-five minutes north of Corpus Christi. A football coach and his team rallied to help their community in need—an encouraging tale that offered hope and the heartwarming belief that no matter what befalls a community, heroes will show up to help. Coach Jason Herring described how much the town had to endure and what they would face moving forward:

> It's a shame there's not a manual for how to deal with the hurricane after the hurricane because I'm going to be honest with you, I've never been through one. And the hurricane after the hurricane is 10 times worse than—a thousand times worse than the hurricane itself.[3]

Coach Herring's insight reminded those who read about him that natural disasters provide opportunities for citizens to do right by one another and to testify to hope and personal triumph—but that's only part of the story. He also reminded people that disasters are complicated, overwhelming, and fraught with tragedy.

The circumstances of Hurricane Harvey, its meteorological idiosyncrasies, and its enormity demand our attention. The giant storm and its aftermath remind us to be ever vigilant in our preparation, readiness, and organization, because storms like this have happened before and *will* happen again. Natural disasters constitute a significant portion of the memories in our nation's scrapbook of pain and suffering, having been burned into the minds of the millions who have experienced devastation and lived to tell about it. We certainly wish that all survivors of natural disasters would both want and be able to return to their destroyed communities, ready to rebuild and face the next challenge, but that has not been, and will not be, everyone's narrative.

Social and Spatial Disparities

When facing natural disasters, some people (who live in certain areas) have access to deep and broad social support networks: services that provide critical aid, circumstances that improve response times and recovery efforts, and processes that facilitate returning everyone and everything to "normal." Yet for others, the rebound is more complicated. For them, recovery is slower, resources are lacking, and social support is all but absent. Of course, we cannot always pinpoint the spatial distinctions that help to shape response and recovery; however, during our research, the stories people told often highlighted some significant differences that emerged with regards to how place and the social fabric of place were important markers of how those people experienced Harvey and its aftermath.

The most notable spatial disparities tend to be those found in the inner city, where the landscape can look dramatically different than the idyllic suburb located a few miles down the interstate. These urban islands are often food deserts serving as containers for the dispossessed and homeless. They also suffer from fractured service networks and can become residences of last resort for impoverished minorities and elders aging-in-place.[4]

The urban residential environment is spatially structured in a way that exposure to risk and even protection against risk varies significantly across neighborhoods. Additionally, the social resources and relationships necessary to address the immediate consequences of such risks are also distributed differentially across social groups located in a city's various neighborhoods.[5] Differential distribution has a profound impact on the health and well-being of communities and its residents. This distribution and its ill-formed processes form a backdrop for some of the stories we heard about Hurricane Harvey from its survivors. Ultimately, Hurricane Harvey was a human-made disaster that clearly amplified existing structural inequalities along the coast.

People's level of preparedness, the resilience of their neighborhoods, and the speed of disaster recovery constituted parts of the varied narrative that we collected from one geographic location to the next along the Texas Gulf Coast. This variance was not a new phenomenon, but rather a story we hear time after time. The most vulnerable—living in the most physically and socially insecure places—are impacted the hardest, have the fewest resources to rely on, and occupy the most unstable neighborhoods post-disaster. Previous research highlights how patterns of racial, ethnic, and income segregation amplify the unequal distribution of opportunity and resources amid the recovery process.[6] The research further underscores how both geographic location and the social characteristics embedded in these locations capture the not-so-pretty picture of a structured inequality that is magnified when natural disasters strike.

In the pages that follow, a story of heartache, destruction, recovery, resilience, and hope unfolds. Funded by the National Science Foundation (NSF), we deployed a team of interviewers all along the Texas Gulf Coast from Corpus Christi to Galveston to talk with survivors and gather their stories. We focus our storytelling lens on how response and recovery looked for people depending on *who they were* and *where they lived*. Through 316 interviews (a combination of both face-to-face and online) and more than forty extended narratives, we make every effort to represent a cross-section of diverse people and places impacted along the Gulf Coast. We also wanted to ensure that the interviews represented different displacement paths, covering a range of choices that people made when the storm began to bear down. This included people who evacuated to shelters, hotels, and alternative locations.

The power of place for everyday experiences and behavior is undeniable. It is key in shaping our life experiences, particularly in times of natural disaster. Some towns had no idea what was coming, while others were prepared to bear the full brunt of the storm. As a result, the stories we have recorded are as complicated and diverse as the residents who lived in these places when Hurricane Harvey made landfall at the end of August 2017.

Our Focus

The central question we ask in the following pages is: *How do place and race intersect in the response to and recovery from a natural disaster?* To answer this question, we examine how social organization impacts recovery, since place and space are critical aspects of all social structures. Related to this central question, we ask a series of sub-questions that provide much of the backdrop for a discussion of response and recovery as we glean insights from interviews and personal narratives offered by individual survivors. Much like a movie script or storyboard, we want to follow this story with a number of interwoven elements from the pre-disaster (preparation), disaster (response), and post-disaster (recovery) sequence of events. A "what's next?" approach seems a fitting way to describe this process, both in terms of the communities that were impacted and the surviving residents' experiences. As we move through each disaster phase, we consider how the underlying social characteristics of place help to describe the individual survivor's experience, the organizations they relied on during the response and early recovery, the communities they lived in, and even the public policies they looked toward for solutions to the messy processes of recovery and rebuilding. Somehow, we need to prevent inefficient and ineffective disaster response and recovery from repeating itself like some perpetual *Groundhog Day*.

Why a Place-Based Perspective for Understanding Disaster?

Place is a critical part of our identity. Who we are is directly connected to the places we live and the spaces we control. These places can range from nations and states to neighborhoods and their dwelling units. All of these different locations have profound social meaning for us, and in a literal sense, they define not only who we are, but also how we live. Ultimately, location also determines the differential risks and benefits we experience.

For some population subgroups, being in the wrong place is not a matter of timing or accident, *but rather a function of social structure*. The places where we live, work, and play are critical resources, just like time or money. Access to these resources dramatically impacts our personal well-being, as well as the overall well-being of the communities in which we live. Pictures are worth a thousand words, and the images that came out of the Gulf Coast region during and after Hurricane Harvey demonstrated that not everyone took the same displacement path or experienced similar roads to recovery. These pictures also told us a lot about the resilience of some communities and the preparedness they had in place well before the storm struck. In contrast, there were some communities that were not prepared at all.

While place and social environment are essential to understanding health and well-being outcomes in society, they are rather broad, multidimensional constructs. Place can be defined as a portion of space regarded as measured off or distinct from other spaces: a specific, geographic, physical location that has distinct boundaries of demarcation. The social environment, on the other hand, can be thought of as the totality of conditions that intersects in a specific place: an area characterized by the social, cultural, economic, and political forces that are constantly intersecting and interacting to create a uniquely identifiable space. Both concepts imply some degree of force, which is physical, but also much more than that. As an environment, a place can be seen as a container whose characteristics derive primarily from what is contained within certain boundaries, including, but not limited to, physical, cultural, political, economic, and social components.

As a portion of space, spatial coordinates can define a place—hence its physical qualities and boundaries. But it is also space, which is socially, culturally, economically, politically, and psychologically constructed. Places occupied by individuals are physical entities characterized by physical positions in space, as well as the characteristics of those elements contained within the spaces. We live in personal worlds, so the same places may be understood and defined very differently by persons with different sociocultural backgrounds and personal experiences. One person's heaven may be another person's hell. Understanding the relationship between social context and well-being thus requires a careful analysis of environments in all their complexity, for place is a multidimensional construct.[7]

This complexity of space and place is certainly important in the context of any natural disaster. The environmental justice, resilience, health and well-being, disaster preparedness, and racial disparities literatures all point to the importance of place and disaster with the clear-as-a-bell adage that not all places are created, maintained, or recovered equally.[8] Numerous works have been written, most recently since Hurricane Katrina, spotlighting the failure of the US government to effectively address the pervasive social inequality in disaster preparedness and resilience development across racially diverse and income-challenged communities. That lack of commitment and decisiveness continues to have disproportionate impact on these neighborhoods—Houston as the most recent example. Studies suggest that racial/ethnic and income disparities regarding the distribution of flooding impact is critical to correcting the environmental injustice that repeats itself every time a natural disaster befalls this country.[9]

Certain population subgroups are exposed to disproportionate amounts of risk because of the places they live and work; likewise, natural disaster survivors are at risk physically, mentally, and economically, and are impacted at much higher rates than their counterparts because of the places they live and work. Mounting evidence suggests that pre-Harvey social patterns in many of the metropolitan spaces along the Texas Gulf Coast were important to influencing decisions that residents made about their evacuation plans and displacement paths. In addition, these patterns helped to determine how residents and their communities would cope during the disaster, as well as how quickly they would recover, rebuild, and prepare for the next natural disaster.

Just like New Orleans,[10] Houston and its surrounding metropolitan spaces knew a disaster was coming. The only question was when. Also like New Orleans, Houston—with its pattern of historical racial and economic segregation—showed very similar signs of socially differentiated preparedness, response, and recovery before, during, and after the Harvey disaster. If developing and maintaining community resilience is the pathway to mitigating place-based disasters that continue to form along social, economic, cultural, and political divisions, then much work needs to be done in the high-risk disaster zone cities of America. Studies now emerging about Houston and Hurricane Harvey show that socially vulnerable groups, including the physically disabled, were residing in neighborhoods with higher proportions of flooded areas at the time of the storm.[11] Flooding and devastation were noted to be significantly higher in neighborhoods predominantly occupied by black, Hispanic, and low-income residents. While those micro-level neighborhood effects are not examined here, the data we collected clearly shows significant health and well-being differences spread across the metropolitan area in part tied to place, and in part tied to displacement strategy, access to resources, and socioeconomic standing. Levels of preparedness and resilience continue to be a vital part of the natural disaster story we tell using the responses and narratives from the survivors.

Like recovery and response, resilience is part of this unequal distribution of resources equation. How prepared communities and their residents are for an impending disaster is not accidental but purposeful. It is tied to the investment that people make in preparation, the resources they leverage to develop strategies, the complex systems of response that are in place, and ultimately the social, human, and economic capital that can be utilized in the development of programs to elicit a direct response.

One federal disaster strategy, known as Whole Community disaster management that started under the Obama administration and has carried into the Trump administration, emphasizes that local communities should be more actively involved in all phases of disaster management, making a place-based approach to understanding disasters even more crucial. While the US federal government is certainly not saying "You're on your own," the Whole Community disaster management approach stresses that *you*—the town's local fire department, the county's public health department, and individual residents themselves—need to play a more active role in disaster preparation, response, and recovery. The magnitude and scope of disasters has left the federal government admitting they can't handle the aftermath on their own. As part of this approach to disasters, FEMA looks to engage and empower local communities. However, the ability to effectively engage and empower residents can vary considerably from one place to another. It is hard to feel empowered or self-reliant when you are already struggling to make ends meet. For those living in communities with limited support and strained resources, a crumbling infrastructure, and very few options for rebuilding or returning, the future can look bleak, and an emphasis on self-reliance confirms feelings of neglect and detachment that existed well before the disaster ever arrived. One anonymous survivor told us in March 2018, "I might as well just forget about returning to my old neighborhood. No one cared or supported us much before the hurricane hit. I doubt they will care about what happens to the neighborhood or us in the weeks and months ahead."

This survivor's statement, expressed amid pain, highlights how the transition from a government-centric plan to a Whole Community plan is far from complete. The survivor does not sound empowered or engaged, but rather feels abandoned. And if enough survivors share this view, recovery will be painfully slow, if not impossible. A place-based approach can help shine a light on the capabilities as well as the limitations that exist to truly engage a whole community in disaster planning, response, and recovery.

Our intention for this book is to bring into focus the important interplay between geography, well-being, disaster response, recovery, and resilience. All of these elements are impacted such that the experience of disaster, displacement, and recovery looks markedly different for people living in Houston than it does for those living in Port Arthur. Likewise, those living in downtown Houston had a strikingly different set of experiences than the residents of Pearland—part of suburban Houston and hard-hit Harris County. Recent work examining the way that different kinds of capital are distributed and utilized during and immediately following a disaster points to significant differences across the metropolitan landscape as well.[12] The findings show rural and urban places losing capital differently while often gaining it through similar forces, though social capital gains were higher in rural areas than urban ones. This, of course, reinforces what we and others have continued to underscore regarding the role of physical place and social space differences and how assets and resilience are not equally distributed in disaster-prone communities. We explore some of these differences in later chapters.

As suggested earlier, place is a function of social structure, and as such, segregation is an important expression of that social structure. This relationship is a vital part of the backdrop necessary for understanding just how important place can be to persons trying to recover from the trauma and distress of disasters like Hurricane Harvey. Residential segregation reproduces inequality for residents, creating difficulty for accessing resources that are necessary to get ahead and stay ahead; with limited access, fragile formal support systems can easily crumble during a natural disaster. America remains a nation divided. Residential location for centuries has accentuated this division and whether white or nonwhite, Hispanic or non-Hispanic, young or old, rich or poor, our communities and neighborhoods have been physically, socially, politically, and economically divided. These divisions are often highlighted during natural disasters. Hurricanes Katrina, Harvey, Irma, and Maria provide us with recent examples where place highlighted the significant variation in pathways of displacement and recovery for residents. Images of the Ninth Ward in New Orleans and videos from Houston's urban neighborhoods have shown us that inequality has a lingering effect on how displacement and recovery differ for residents during and after a natural disaster.

We argue in this book that displacement, well-being, response, and recovery are all subject to the wildly variable disparities across metropolitan spaces; place, status, race, and social structure are woven into a fabric that tells a distinctive part of the Hurricane Harvey survivor's story. While our intention is to shine a spotlight on this "place effect," we are also keenly aware of the important role that poverty plays in determining health and well-being, particularly among those persons living in highly dense, minority-concentrated neighborhoods. We believe these structural characteristics impact not only individual well-being, but also community well-being and resilience. Though often not included in the recovery conversation, poverty, inequality, and segregation need to be part of the next generation's disaster management agenda. We must address racial and economic discrimination and the role it plays in impeding preparedness, survival, and recovery.[13] So, what then is the context for the story we want to tell?

Context Matters: The Natural Disaster Impact

The history of natural disasters in the United States over the last hundred years has been a complicated and powerful one—shaping the destiny of millions of people, thousands of communities, hundreds of organizations, and one country. Scholars often define natural disasters as major disruptions to the social structure, failures of the social system, and the cataclysmic intertwining of social systems with natural hazards. Houston and large cities like it that have experienced massive concrete development with little planning for natural disasters provide telling examples of how these two forces—natural and human-made—collide to create the power and lasting impact of disasters like Hurricane Harvey.

Typically, natural disasters represent large-scale traumatic events that disrupt the routine of daily living and threaten the self-sufficiency of a society, often with unspeakable consequences.[14] Large-scale devastation means the loss of life, property, and community that can shake a society at its core. Natural disasters are especially problematic when they strike locations with susceptible physical and social infrastructures that are ill-prepared or ill-equipped to absorb the full impact of such a devastating blow. Even as well-equipped as the United States may appear to be, large-scale natural disasters like Hurricane Harvey can have significant, immediate impact on the smaller, less-prepared places like Rockport or Refugio, Texas, where the long-term negative health and safety consequences linger for months and even years afterward.

Precisely, these are the circumstances that make it difficult to effectively develop mediation strategies to help compensate for the unimaginable impact disasters have on people and property. Beyond uprooting entire social structures and family systems, natural disasters can impact the social, economic, political, and health balance of places in the blink of an eye. What once stood tall in a community can be wiped away, leaving nothing but a foundation behind. Natural disasters can strike quickly, seemingly picking targets at random, and leaving some places digging out from under the massive rubble. Some will rebuild with a focus on resilience, while other places will struggle their entire post-disaster existence to shake off the heavy cloak of destruction and despair.

The specific consequences of disaster often vary from one event to another, but some consistent aftereffects are commonly experienced by communities. These consequences were certainly evident in many Texas Gulf Coast communities after Hurricane Harvey.

1) *The physical and mental health fabric of towns and cities on the Texas Gulf Coast was ripped apart.* Besides the loss of life, hundreds

of people were injured. People streamed into urgent care centers and emergency rooms all along the Gulf Coast, arriving with problems from broken limbs and waterborne illnesses to severe anxiety, post-traumatic stress, and overall malaise. Though drowning is a massive risk amid a hurricane, residents were exposed to a number of secondary health risks because of the storm surge, high winds, and general destructive power of Hurricane Harvey. Everyone is vulnerable to disaster stress, both during and after an event like this one; our measures of mental health and physical health symptoms among the residents we interviewed showed a heightened sensitivity to the power of this storm. When residents are uprooted from their homes and forced to evacuate to hotels, shelters, or even locations in another city, their coping strategies are disrupted, their social resource networks are diminished, and even their physiological responses are impacted. Hurricane Harvey survivors experienced this triple threat, and these effects—though not always referred to as such—are part of their stories.

2) *The social resource network and social capital in the towns and cities on the Texas Gulf Coast were disrupted.* When disaster breaches the social fabric of a community, everything residents once depended on or felt secure about disappears. Then survivors have to quickly pick up the pieces and repair the now-torn social fabric. In addition to the informal social networks that are impacted by natural disasters, formal social networks and resource systems that are critical partners in the recovery process are directly affected too. While these organizations are committed to helping survivors piece together a plan for next steps, they often find themselves picking up their own pieces and cobbling together an organization that can serve and operate in the worst of circumstances. Health care, education, transportation, social services, legal services, and criminal justice agencies are all impacted by natural disasters, and their capacity to effectively serve survivors is often threatened.

Beyond the negative impact on the formal social resource and support networks that many of the Texas coastal communities faced, what impact did Hurricane Harvey have on local friendship networks, social ties, and the social capital in these communities? Seemingly overnight, as is common amid disasters, many Hurricane Harvey survivors lost touch with their neighbors, friends, and even family. Communication networks were compromised, people were displaced from their homes, and residents had to evacuate so quickly that they had little or no opportunity to tell each other if they were leaving or staying put.

Additionally, we wanted to know what happens to these social networks and informal sources of social connectedness during or after a disaster. Would these connections ever be rebuilt, like the homes and communities people occupy? Would new social connections emerge? We were interested in exploring these questions in more detail with the survivors we met. In the time that we spent in the Houston area during the training and deployment of interviewers, and later on in Galveston at the conclusion of the interviewing, we had several serendipitous opportunities to see and hear firsthand how some people dealt with tragedy and coped with loss. By the end of our research, we better understood how integral informal social networks could be to the newly scripted version of life after a disaster.

3) *The economic and political infrastructures in the towns and cities on the Texas Gulf Coast were compromised.* Estimates are still coming in, but by the majority of accounts, Hurricane Harvey will have a price tag in excess of 130 billion dollars. When the final bill is paid, and the final restitution check is sent out, this will be one of the costliest hurricanes in modern history, second only to Hurricane Katrina; nearly three times the amount of money will be spent on repairs, improvements, construction, etc., than was spent in other large-scale disasters. While federal and state support for cleanup is vital, particularly to smaller cities and towns, local economies will have to bear some of that financial burden. In some cases, they will be unable to absorb such financial blows.

A disaster's immediate impact is obvious, but perhaps even more painful for some of these places will be the long-term impact on their economic development. Coastal towns that rely on seasonal attraction may experience years-long financial consequences as they wait for vacationers to return. Until they do return, the boardwalks need to be rebuilt, sand dunes must be replaced, hotels and condominiums will undergo extensive repair, and small businesses will need time to reboot. In the other cities and towns along the Texas Gulf Coast, residents are still trying to put the pieces of their lives back together to achieve a "new normal"—getting their children back in school and returning to work. Of course, life carries on while those same small-town residents wait for construction materials, financial assistance, and repairs to be made on their homes, businesses, churches, and schools. Billions of dollars were set aside for relief, but so far, only millions of dollars have been spent.

Consider for a minute how a disaster creates a domino effect that has economic implications for a community's ability to recover in the short- and long-term. On August 17, 2018, in an interview with NPR, Port Arthur Mayor Derrick Freeman estimated that Harvey had damaged 80 percent of the city's structures. The first domino had fallen. As finger pointing and feet dragging ensued among lawmakers in Austin and Washington, funding to fix the overwhelming property damage stalled, and residents were left waiting to return to their hometown. The second domino fell. Fear emerged in Port Arthur that those who evacuated anticipating a temporary exit now faced a permanent exit from their community as the residents pondered the difficult financial and emotional question of whether it would even be worth it to rebuild. Certainly, a permanent exit would impact a community's ability to reopen businesses, fill jobs, and rebuild the local economy. A third domino fell. Reports in spring 2018 revealed an almost 10 percent decline in Port Arthur's population following Harvey, with concerns that if such a decline continued into the 2020 census, the community would lose out on critical resources made available from the federal government.[15] Another domino would fall.

Port Arthur's experiences demonstrate how the economic impact of Harvey will reverberate throughout the Texas Gulf Coast for years to come and in ways that have not been fully anticipated. Again, we are provided with another example of how geographic place is intertwined with our understanding of response and recovery. The size of a place is an important driver in this push to recover faster and stronger. Nevertheless, limited social resources, a limited core of residents and businesses, and limited capital can slow the recovery process.[16]

When a natural disaster strikes a concentrated area like the southeastern Gulf Coast of Texas, government at every level is impacted. FEMA and the Small Business Administration (SBA) must initiate financial transactions to address recovery that will take place at every level. The sheer number of affected residents taxes the overall political infrastructure. When in response mode, the government assists directly in cleanup, meets immediate health care needs, helps indirectly by providing necessary workspaces, or temporarily suspends specific laws or regulations in order to speed up the repair and revival of damaged communities. Though the goal is for government to help rather than hinder, this type of frenzied, active response can become taxing to organizations and the people who work for them.

Disaster victims eventually realize that recovery feels more like a marathon than a sprint, but the demand from survivors generally overwhelms the stamina of the staff of assistance organizations. It's hard to explain that to people who have been waiting for months to talk with FEMA representatives, insurance adjustors, contractors, and others upon whom survivors rely to help them put their lives back together.

4) *The ecology and natural landscapes in the towns and cities on the Texas Gulf Coast were physically altered.* Heavy winds, extreme flooding, and storm surges pack so much power that they can change the land itself in the blink of an eye. The flooding in Houston destroyed natural barriers and uprooted thousands of trees and bushes, forcing wild mammals, birds, amphibians, and insects out of their natural habitats. Of course, countless creatures across the species spectrum were destroyed and a natural selection process, much like that which takes place during forest fires, droughts, and other natural disasters, rearranged the ecology of Houston and its outlying coastal areas. Whooping cranes arrived in Port Aransas, Texas, from Canada in early winter to find a devastated landing point—a new ecological imbalance that will have serious implications for the nesting population and future generations. This example is but one of numerous ecological microdisasters that have befallen the Texas Gulf Coast region since the arrival of Hurricane Harvey.

It's All about Timing: 2017, the Weather Year from Hell

The year 2017 was branded by media images of disaster. Evening newscasts, both local and national, peppered viewers with stories, pictures, and interviews for weeks and months, natural disaster after natural disaster. In the early part of 2017, flooding in California and tornado outbreaks in the southern and midwestern parts of the United States dominated the news cycle. By the time Hurricane Harvey made landfall in late August, we had become a country numbed by weather and climate disasters that cost the United States billions of dollars.

Hurricanes Harvey, Irma, and Maria left an indelible stamp of sorrow on our country. With over 3,167 lives lost and costs exceeding 275 billion dollars, 2017 was a year to remember and a year we all want to forget.[17] By the year's end—with massive fires, mudslides, and torrential rains in Southern California over the holiday season—the National Centers for Environmental Information (NCEI) had recorded as many as sixteen billion-dollar-plus weather and climate disasters for the year in the United States. To contextualize these storms and their severity: collectively, the disasters of 2017 constituted the most expensive natural and climate disaster calendar year in recorded history, shattering the previous record held by 2005 when Hurricanes Dennis, Katrina, Rita, and Wilma found their way to the southeastern coastal regions of the United States.

What made 2017 so prone to disaster? Speculation and debate continue, but we do know that 2017 was nearly three degrees warmer than the average temperature recorded at any time during the twentieth century. Likewise, summer 2017 was the second-hottest season on record since the late 1800s. This heat, of course, helped to fuel wildfires and intensify hurricanes.

Climatologists have been claiming all along that the types of changes they're observing, and the frequency with which they're observing them, point toward an uptick in disaster-level events.[18] So we actually asked Hurricane Harvey survivors what they thought about climate change and its role in the disaster they experienced. A community can only be resilient if it identifies and understands the risks that it faces. Thus, the resilience of the Texas Gulf Coast to recover, rebuild, and prepare for future hurricanes like Harvey will be in question if those residents, who we argue are survivors of a climate-related event, still view climate change as a distant threat with little relevance to their personal lives. We will delve more deeply into conversations about climate change and survivors' perceptions of climate change later in the book.

It isn't complicated; climate change is confounding our world's weather, making storms more frequent and severe. While climate change continues to be a divisive political issue, an overwhelming majority of the scientific community has carefully detailed its causal structure and diverse set of consequences with a fair amount of certainty. One thing we know for sure: Harvey was one of the worst storms in US history, and it was fueled by a warmer-than-usual Gulf of Mexico. Harvey was a disaster waiting to happen.[19]

Because Harvey was a weather system that stalled, it was able to dump enormous amounts of water in a concentrated area. Some scientists blamed that stall on a shrinking polar ice cap, which reduced the strength of the polar jet stream. The polar jet stream can weaken the atmospheric steering currents that typically dip down and disrupt storms like Harvey—currents that would, under typical conditions, either prevent the storms from forming altogether or make them considerably less violent.[20] As climate science highlights the increasing demands being placed on our cities and towns around the country, we also know that most cities have not been built or engineered to account for the negative consequences of climate change.

Houston is the perfect example of a city that continues to grow while ignoring the climate change threat—sprawling slowly, adding more concrete, and building more dams. We heard plenty of stories when talking with Harvey survivors about how water seemingly had no place to go—and that much of the damage occurred when water was released from dams that otherwise would have broken. After lawsuits appeared in state and federal court, we learned that when those dams released water under city order, they flooded and destroyed neighborhoods downstream that were both unprepared and unprotected. The waters rose and moved with a force and speed that inundated the communities.

No doubt, 2017 will be remembered as an epic weather year, not only by scientists and meteorologists, but also by survivors who lost loved ones, pets, personal belongings, and homes. As outsiders, we found nothing about telling this story of displacement and destruction to be simple; so many different angles, sub-plots and twists, actors, and scenery changes informed the narrative. Thus, in order to guide the reader, we want to offer a brief overview of the chapters ahead. We don't know how the story will end, since some survivors will be recovering for years to come, but we do hope the data, interviews, and insight we've collected here will arm future researchers with information and help local communities and the government to sharpen their response. Ultimately, we hope the next storm will not claim as many victims or cost as much time or money as Hurricane Harvey did.

A Framework for the Book

As we have discussed, an important set of social relationships intersects in physical place, making this story more complicated than mere social or economic inequality. For many places, residential segregation became an important part of the story right away, predetermining and limiting the pathways of displacement available to coastal residents. One must acknowledge the history of power, race, and place in order to understand the modern town and city in America, and when we examine towns and cities amid natural disasters, something crystallizes. What emerges is a frank and compelling story about poverty, racial injustice, and historical discrimination.[21] The structural circumstances of US cities and towns have real and meaningful consequences for the well-being of residents and communities.[22] We would expect those consequences to be compounded in places that have been living in the grip of the threat, or experiencing firsthand the distress that comes with natural disasters. Prior research provides us with a glimpse of this "effect," as authors told the story of how Katrina revealed its own brand of ugliness in New Orleans—an ugliness we knew existed but had not fully perceived until we saw the national news broadcasting images that needed no caption.[23]

Hurricane Harvey was not an isolated event but rather one more example in a long list of historical disasters that remind us that health, well-being, and resilience are intertwined elements crucial to our understanding of the power of place. Throughout this book, we examine nuances of the Hurricane Harvey story and the circumstances that led to one of the costliest natural disasters in US history. While our intent is to tell this story through the words and responses of Harvey survivors, we also want to weave their words of experience into the broader interrelationships between place, race, displacement, resilience, social capital, and recovery.

Chapter two describes the process of developing and executing the project. We believe it is crucial to explain how we obtained the data and to describe how difficult it was to gain the organizational cooperation that would provide the needed access. The Red Cross was protective, FEMA had its hands tied, and churches were so overwhelmed with requests and immediate crisis management that our need to gain access to survivors nearly got lost in the shuffle. Chapter two describes the framework used to select persons for both our face-to-face interviews and online surveys, along with the follow-up strategies we employed to talk with civilians and organizational officials involved in the recovery process. The chapter also describes both our approach to data collection and the specific data we hoped to acquire as it pertained to understanding how displacement and recovery processes varied from individual to individual. Finally, we discuss the strategies we employed to tell the survivors' stories—pictures, maps, tables, charts, narratives, and additional data from secondary sources that helped us characterize the places where survivors lived, both before and after the disaster.

Chapter three presents a visual characterization of the disaster. Using mapping and other visual aids, this chapter describes the region, the impacted communities, and the locations and characteristics of the disaster survivors. A number of important questions are addressed in this chapter, including: What were the sociodemographic and socioeconomic aggregate profiles of the affected communities, and how were those profiles related to the pathway of displacement and recovery for the survivors? Also, what were the socio-spatial characteristics of specific outcomes among survivors (e.g., displacement options, attitudes about disruption and destruction, resilience perceptions, etc.)?

The middle section of our story takes an important descriptive shift. Chapters four, five, and six provide an in-depth examination of the chronology of events and the underlying circumstances of preparedness, response, and short-term recovery related to Hurricane Harvey. Specifically, we were interested in asking residents how prepared or ill-prepared they were, how directly or indirectly they were impacted, and how they experienced and are still experiencing recovery. The comprehensive nature of the data we collected provides important insight into the phases of this natural disaster, the varying responses to decisions about displacement, and the coping mechanisms survivors employed in the face of the grim reality of having lost everything or seeing their neighbors lose everything. Our intent is to create running narratives through each of these chapters to help illuminate the varying phases of the disaster from the survivors' perspectives.

Chapter four examines the background of this disaster in a chronological way. Questions we pose in this chapter include: Where did Hurricane Harvey survivors live before the hurricane made landfall? What did survivors' social networks look like prior to the disaster? To what groups and community organizations did survivors belong? How did survivors describe where they lived? How prepared were they and their neighbors? What was the general tone of public disaster communication? Which groups knew what, and how was that information disseminated to different communities? Were these communities gearing up for serious risk assessment? The answers to these questions and more outline the shapes of people's experiences during the storm.

Chapter five examines the natural disaster event itself and how survivors assessed their situations during that period of trauma and terror. What did residents' displacement processes look like? How did where they lived affect those processes? What defined the displacement story for people who relied on various strategies to evacuate after the hurricane hit (i.e., going to shelters, moving into a hotel, living with friends and families, etc.)? How did survivors feel about the adequacy of the disaster response (support from their neighbors, community support, the organizations in place to provide aid and assistance) and the government agencies expected to guide them through recovery? Their responses are insightful, and once again they drive home the importance of understanding how these experiences varied by displacement pathway, place of residence, and severity of damage.

Chapter six examines the post-event sequence and the circumstances of short-term recovery. How did survivors adjust to life, weeks, and months after the storm? How did they cope in the aftermath of Harvey? In particular, what was the epidemiology of disaster mental health following this event? What social and economic factors may have exacerbated challenging mental health reactions? How have survivors found meaning amid the damage and destruction? Do those perceptions differ across communities and across types of displacement? How did this natural disaster experience influence survivors' views on climate change? Have survivors changed their attitudes toward disasters and preparedness? Have their Hurricane Harvey experiences affected those attitudes, or are Texas Gulf Coast residents doomed to repeat the same mistakes? The answers to these questions further support what we suspected all along: that not everyone's experiences were the same, and that how they reported or recalled their experiences correlates to who they were and where they lived.

Chapter seven provides some practical prevention and intervention strategies, formulated for individual citizens, civic organizations, and local governments at risk for experiencing natural disasters. Each subsection offers best-practice preventions/interventions to be used when discussing disaster preparedness and capacity-building in communities. This chapter explores elements critical to our general understanding of the complicated processes of disaster and recovery. We draw from the stories we collected and the data we gathered to identify community strengths that could be channeled to reduce the negative impact on individuals and communities when the next hurricane hits. We also reflect on what our role should be as "disaster citizens," even if we don't live in communities that are prone to natural disasters like hurricanes.

Social connectedness among survivors is key. We examine the diversity that hurricane survivors reported regarding their organizational memberships, complex social networks, and connectedness to neighbors. Such social resources are crucial when disasters strike. We underscore the importance of informal and formal citizen disaster communication in augmenting formal disaster relief efforts, and examine proposed preventions/interventions that might be useful when it comes to relying on social connections both before and after a natural disaster.[24]

Recognizing the need for a community-care approach, we examined the role of health and well-being among populations at risk for natural disasters. The intersection of place and mental health is an important part of any risk assessment, and being sensitive to high-risk targets and the effects this may have on these groups before, during, and after a natural disaster is an important consideration. As such, we discuss some preventions/interventions in the context of the role of well-being and mental health in the pre- and post-disaster period.

Finally, we underscore the importance of displacement and the pathways that are forced upon some survivors based on who they were or where they lived. Disasters can highlight the extraordinary inequalities across communities and neighborhoods and how those inequalities impact displacement options and strategies. We examine these strategies in detail and note that the longer and more convoluted the displacement process is, the greater the impact on both residents and the larger community. In this chapter, we ask: What pathways did survivors utilize for normalizing life and returning to school, church, and work?

In summary, our goal for this book is straightforward: to document, through the words of survivors and the data they generated, how the complicated natural disaster process impacts populations and places differently. Like most stories, this one doesn't take place in a vacuum, and we hope readers will come to better appreciate the multi-stranded social, economic, political, demographic, and cultural fabric woven into the survivors' words.

2

Who We Are

When we first arrived in Houston on the morning of October 11, 2017, we were cautiously optimistic as we prepared to launch our National Science Foundation (NSF) project. The project promised to be unlike any research we had ever done. Writing the original proposal, receiving funding, and arriving—boots on the ground to train interviewers—had all taken place in less than two months. The compressed timeline meant we needed to move efficiently to ensure our resources were in place and to recruit and train our interviewers. Amid the lingering chaos of a natural disaster zone, we employed a strategy for acquiring as many interviews as possible in a short amount of time.

In a story, subplots support the main narrative; amid our research, one subplot of particular interest was uncovering, in broad terms, how people faced this disaster. If they evacuated, they had different pathways for getting out of harm's way—which is an important part of the story. If they chose to stay, how were their situations or outcomes different from those who could not stay or were forced to evacuate? We wanted answers to more questions: Who went off in different directions, chose different survival strategies, and anticipated different outcomes? How can we characterize these people? Are they as different as we think? Do respondents' outlooks for the future differ depending on where they lived or how they chose to deal with the storm?

Given our focus and interest in these issues, we needed to collect many different types of responses from survivors in order to get a clear, broad understanding of the experiences and circumstances for survivors and their families before, during, and after the storm's arrival. In addition to the relevant questions about sociodemographics, family history, and residential history, we compiled major areas of inquiry that required sets of questions to tap into specific areas. These response topics included physical and mental health, social networks and social support, social capital, attitudes about community resilience and preparedness, perspectives on the future, and specific plans for recovery and rebuilding that individuals made during the post-disaster period. Regardless of our own preparedness, our task was not going to be easy.

You Want to Talk about What?

Who would ever assume that interviewing hurricane survivors—just weeks after their entire lives had been uprooted—would be easy? A few days into our visit, as we drove around some of these neighborhoods, we better understood how the location's chaotic circumstances would present major challenges to completing this work. Yet we were determined to locate survivors and listen to them talk about their experiences, to make sense of their current situations, to learn something about their backgrounds, and to assess their overall health and well-being post-disaster. Our knowledge of fieldwork had been mixed, and neither one of us had any extensive experience working *on-site* with natural disaster populations so close to the timing of the event.

We had, however, designed and executed surveys in a variety of challenging settings and knew how hard it could be to find and interview difficult-to-reach populations (i.e., homeless adults, youth living in high-risk neighborhoods, abortion clinic workers, and even natural disaster survivors). The major difference between those experiences and this project was the necessary immediacy: we needed to interview survivors as soon as possible, in places still classified as disaster/recovery zones. Also unlike our work in the past, we really had no built-in network of providers or survivors to help us meet potential respondents and accomplish the task at hand. Nevertheless, we were both up to the challenge. Matthew, a communication researcher with specific interest in natural disasters, understood the extraordinary value of accessing natural disaster survivors at the beginning of the recovery process. Kevin, a sociologist with interests in the intersection of race, place, and health, hoped for an opportunity to explore this nexus in a disaster setting, which he had never done before. We both understood what an important opportunity this was; yet we also recognized the importance of being respectful and careful as we approached groups and individuals during this time of grief, anxiety, and for many, desperation.

We knew working in a natural disaster site would be challenging, but we were unprepared for what the fieldwork would demand. For many of these potential interviewees, their lives as they knew them no longer existed. Their houses were gone, their neighbors were gone, and for some, their communities were destroyed. They had been displaced and then resettled in a hundred different directions. Figuring out where these survivors had landed would be the first task, but we then had to determine who to interview and where to geographically focus those interviews (counties, cities, zip code areas, neighborhoods, etc.). Then we needed to consider how to best meet the project goals by pinpointing what we really wanted to learn from these survivors once we finally had the opportunity to interview them.

The success of the project hinged on how quickly and efficiently we could train and deploy interviewers into the disaster zones all along the Texas Gulf Coast. What we originally proposed to the NSF was a sound strategy for identifying, recruiting, and interviewing Harvey survivors. However, once we visited Texas and met with survivors and relief workers, we soon realized the flaws in our proposed approach. We had initially planned on going to the agencies most intimately involved in recovery (the Red Cross, FEMA, the Salvation Army, etc.) and soliciting their help recruiting interviewees in the early weeks and months after the hurricane. Once we had gained access to the right locations—up and down the southeastern coast of Texas—we had planned to randomly select interviewees representing the varying population concentrations in specific cities. We had done our due diligence beforehand and talked with the proper agencies and individuals, who had led us to believe they would cooperate. But none of this advance planning worked out as intended.

We hope this will serve as a useful teaching example of how the researcher/scientist imagines what a "best approach" might be in the confines of their laboratory or office, but when it's actually time for the fieldwork, circumstances turn out to be very different. We certainly expected the kinds of challenges that others have reported when working in the field of natural disasters (such as how to identify specific groups of survivors available for interview, find the right times and places to do adequate data collections, and be sensitive to the circumstances that survivors were facing while at the same time needing to talk and interview them in the midst of the disaster).[1] Finding, accessing, and interviewing Hurricane Harvey survivors required many adjustments, midstream corrections, and flexible interviewers willing to shift priorities and change their approach to identifying potential interview candidates.

Finally, we developed a concrete interviewee selection plan: we wanted to talk with a group of survivors that was as representative and random as possible. Accomplishing this task, however, would not happen without a lot of hard, creative work and a group of vigilant interviewers, as well as a set of respondents willing to work around schedules and make accommodations.

Best Laid Plans

The original strategy for obtaining interviews was complicated. As we mapped this out in our offices soon after we had been awarded the funds from the NSF, some critical questions arose: Where should we conduct the interviews, with whom, and from what targeted number of specific locations and population subgroups? Our first step was to identify every county impacted by Hurricane Harvey, with a particular focus on the counties that were hardest hit. What damage estimates were coming in from FEMA? What declarations had been made by local and state governments regarding the number of homes impacted, persons killed and injured, etc.? We needed some answers in order to finalize a strategy for developing interviewee targets.

We also considered which population groups had most likely been impacted, and we wondered if that impact would relate to their exit strategies and/or displacement pathways. Remember, our focus was on the correlation between where people lived at the time Hurricane Harvey hit and their displacement stories. We hoped examining this connection would help us better understand response and recovery outcomes among survivors. As such, an effort was made to identify specific groups of persons who: (a) did not need to evacuate; (b) were forced to evacuate to a public shelter operated by the Red Cross, FEMA, the Salvation Army, etc.; and (c) were forced to evacuate to a hotel/motel or to locations with family/friends. These three distinctive groups represented a primary focus for us in gathering face-to-face interviews, as they represented a broad spectrum of experience and exposure. These groups later helped us focus the gathering of additional interviews from survivors using a targeted online strategy.

Who and How?

Let's take a moment here to describe how we approached securing survivor interviews. Our first step was to examine the counties that were impacted the most based on FEMA's damage estimates, the size of those counties, their racial and ethnic diversity, and the size and diversity characteristics of the larger cities found within each of those counties. As such, our primary targets for doing interviews became the largest population concentrations of Brazoria, Galveston, Harris, Jefferson, and Nueces Counties. Of course, many other counties were impacted by the hurricane, but the counties we targeted had the largest population concentrations with sizable cities (over twenty thousand). We ended up taking the total population estimates from these counties, based on these larger cities (roughly 3.5 million people), and made a series of decisions in anticipation of securing somewhere between 300 and 350 interviews. Part of that decision was based on the realistic expectation of what we could secure with the funds allocated from the NSF, as well as our time limits and the number of interviews our eight trained interviewers could reasonably conduct.

So, for example, we looked at Brazoria County, and with its total city populations of approximately 167,000, the county represented about 5 percent of the total number of persons based on the earlier FEMA estimate of 3.5 million persons directly or indirectly impacted by the hurricane. To maintain that ratio and have Brazoria County represent 5 percent of the total interviews, we estimated we would need at least fourteen interviews from this county. Alvin, Lake Jackson, and Pearland were the specific city targets within Brazoria County, though interviews could also come from persons living elsewhere in the county and outside of any one of these city limits. In addition, we added more to our interview selection criteria. We needed a reasonable gender distribution (preferably 50/50), as well as a distribution that reflected the racial and ethnic composition of the counties of focus. To simplify matters, we focused on obtaining white versus nonwhite interviews, and then once we determined the concentration of Hispanics in each of the targeted cities, we included that into our final computations of how many nonwhite interviews we would need to obtain. Brazoria County's population is 88 percent white, so of the fourteen interviewees, nine would need to be white and five would be nonwhite. Thirty percent of those five nonwhite interviewees (two) would need to be Hispanic (in accordance with Brazoria County's estimate of its Hispanic population). It seems complicated, but we needed our approach to ensure some degree of equal and accurate representation of the impacted population generally, focusing on interviews that reflected the racial and ethnic diversity in those areas as well.

Here is an example of how things actually worked out when it came to our plans for interviewee selection. The data we collected for Brazoria County included twenty-five total interviews (our original target was a minimum of fourteen). Sixty percent of interviewees were women (against an original target of 50 percent). The racial and ethnic targets were fairly precise: 88 percent of interviewees were white, perfectly on target, and we needed at least a third of nonwhite respondents to be Hispanic—we managed 21 percent. Finally, interviews were divided into groups of those not having to move from their residence (58 percent) and the remaining respondents who were displaced (42 percent) divided across the other displacement options. Table 2.1 shows the specific targets that we estimated for interviewing in these selected counties. Keep in mind that these represented targeted estimates, and in some cases, we were successful in reaching the targets. In other cases, we were not.

Two different processes operated simultaneously during the initial data collection period (October 15, 2017, through January 15, 2018). The first part of the project, after the interviewers were trained and deployed, was to have interviewers connect directly with service providers and other organizations responsible for housing and accommodating Harvey survivors. With more than 190 targeted interviews in Harris County, the majority of the interviews that needed to be done immediately were in and around the Houston metropolitan area. Several strategies for recruiting interviewees were initiated: (a) we contacted local shelters and service providers responsible for relocating survivors into temporary housing; (b) we contacted hotels/motels that were primary locations for survivors receiving vouchers from FEMA; (c) using several service providers with large distribution networks, we emailed flyers to potential interviewees to see if anyone would be interested in being interviewed;

TABLE 2.1. Sociodemographics of Selected Counties for Interviewee Targets

	Harris	Nueces	Brazoria	Galveston	Jefferson	Fort Bend	Orange	Aransas	Montgomery
Total									
Gender									
Male	55.9	36.4	40	35	12.5	33.3	6.7	50	80
Female	44.1	63.6	60	65	87.5	66.7	93.3	50	20
Race									
White	68.2	90.9	88	80	87.5	0	20	100	100
Nonwhite	31.8	9.1	12	20	12.5	100	80	0	0
Ethnicity									
Hispanic	31.8	54.5	20.8	20	0	0	0	0	0
Non-Hispanic	68.2	45.5	79.2	80	100	100	100	100	100
Stay									
With a Friend or Relative or Hotel	21.8	6.7	25	11.1	25	0	46.7	0	0
Shelters, Outdoors, or Car	16.5	0	0	0	0	33.3	6.7	0	0
Other	8.5	3	16.7	0	12.5	0	20	0	0
Own Home	53.2	90	58.3	88.9	62.5	66.7	26.7	100	100

and (d) using interviewees as part of a snowball sampling process, we asked interviewees for names and contact information of friends and family impacted by the storm who might also be interested in being interviewed. This was our boots-on-the ground strategy, and it netted approximately one hundred completed face-to-face interviews.

A second method, introduced as a supplement to what we did on the ground, was to contract with a large national research firm, Qualtrics, Inc. They sent out an identical survey to the one we were using in the face-to-face interviews, but Qualtrics built a series of selection protocol questions requiring persons to meet specific criteria in order to participate in the project. Qualtrics first sent the survey out to a targeted set of zip codes that were part of FEMA's county estimates of areas that had received the highest levels of damage. Then, panels of potential respondents were asked questions related to their gender, race, ethnicity, and their displacement pathway (those who stayed in their homes/apartments, those who were displaced to emergency shelters, and/or those who were displaced to hotels/motels or to family's/friends' homes). We mentioned earlier the importance of controlling for displacement where we could so that roughly one-third of our respondents did not evacuate and relocate. Comparing this group—the "no-effect" group—to the others would be an important contrast with respect to their experiences and circumstances. In the end, we collected 316 completed interviews, with two-thirds of these survivors evacuating and being displaced, and one-third staying in their home or apartment.

These mixed-method data collection strategies netted us a higher concentration of interviews in the more urbanized areas along the Texas Gulf Coast. Nevertheless, we were able to secure interviews with survivors who lived in less populous locations, including the outskirts of both Galveston City and Corpus Christi. Both qualitative and quantitative data were gleaned from these interviews.

Welcome to the Real World

Returning to October 11, 2017: our plane landed in the fourth largest city in the United States, a place we had never been before, where we knew no one. It was going to be a whirlwind trip. With only three days to accomplish a great deal of work, we had a full schedule. We needed to train interviewers, meet with FEMA and Red Cross officials, connect with United Way, talk with Salvation Army disaster relief coordinators, and meet with shelter managers, school officials, and homeless service providers.

Houston was on the verge of winning the World Series in 2017, but a cloud of anger, disappointment, frustration, and sadness seemed to hang over the city. Unlike the big hurricanes before it (e.g., Ike, Alicia, Rita), Harvey left behind physical damage that was a lot harder to see. And yet, one could tell that something really big had just happened.

People weren't interested in talking about it—a reluctance we struggled to explain.

After we checked into our hotel that afternoon, we bumped into Alice—our very first survivor who would talk with us. She was anxious to tell us about the circumstances that had landed her at the La Quinta hotel for almost two months after Harvey. As an aside, like all the other survivors we write about in this book, we gave her a pseudonym. The names you see here are not real, but rather names we made up to protect their identities while following the required human subjects protocol provided by the University of Arkansas, our home institution.

Alice had been living in the La Quinta Inn since August 29, and not long after sitting and talking with her in the hotel dining room, we had an aha moment. Alice launched into a long, richly detailed description, recalling her story as it had naturally unfolded. A day or two before Harvey made landfall, Alice and her husband were as prepared as they thought they needed to be. Her husband, nearly eighty years old and somewhat frail, was not much help in the preparation, but Alice was twenty years younger and athletic, commanding, and organized. Her strong handshake and physical gestures convinced us right away that she was the kind of person we'd want to go through a natural disaster with. She gave off an air of confidence that she was ready for whatever nature might throw at her. But what she told us was quite the opposite. She had not been ready for the hurricane, the rainfall, or the events that followed.

Alice and her husband had reluctantly decided to stay in their house. They believed they would be safe, given that it was a multistory home and not located in a high-risk flood zone. They had plenty of provisions, and though the first few days were tense, riding it out went as well as could be expected. She described a lot of water—more water than they'd ever seen in their neighborhood—but she suspected, like her neighbors, that it would eventually recede. Still, the rain continued to pour down, and the water rose and rose in the streets and yards and even in the streets that bordered her Energy Corridor neighborhood. Alice knew they would be trapped soon and the only option left was to wait patiently in their home, on the second floor, until the water disappeared.

She recalled the water rising rapidly in their backyard, and how their dog could no longer go outside after the water crept up the back porch steps. A minor inconvenience, she thought, even joking with her husband that the only way out might be by boat if the rain didn't stop. She never could have known that, after all, they would end up leaving their house by boat with only a few bags of possessions, the dog, and some clothing. They piled into the neighbors' boat—the same neighbors who had checked on them earlier that morning as the water moved in and filled up their first-floor living space. The ten brick steps from their sidewalk path to their front door were now covered, and water flowed into the kitchen and living room like a slow-moving river passing through their house.

Five days after this nightmare started for them, county and city authorities, along with the United States Army Corps of Engineers, made a decision to release water from the Addicks and Barker reservoirs. By the time the water was released, it was too late for many residents, like Alice and her husband, to evacuate; the residents were unprepared when the reservoir waters swamped their downstream neighborhoods along the Buffalo Bayou in the western section of Houston. Overnight, water rushed into the Energy Corridor and Memorial neighborhoods, flooding garages and first floors of every house and condominium in its path. No one received advanced warning about this intentional water release. No one had time to salvage their possessions or even move their cars.

After talking late into that first night, the next morning we took a drive through Alice's neighborhood at her urging to survey the aftermath of what she had described to us the night before. Even nearly two months later, watermarks fifteen feet high were still visible on the sides of homes, fences, and garages, serving as eerie reminders of what had happened there. The water had receded, but the destruction was still visible. Her neighborhood looked like a white dust bomb had exploded, as wallboard dust formed a thin layer over the houses, lawns, garbage piles, and cars. Every street was covered in white film, as if snow had fallen and stuck to the roads. People were cleaning and building at a fevered pitch, and we could hardly drive around all the construction equipment, trucks, and cars parked along the street. Some streets were impassable because of the heavy equipment in place to tear down the sides of homes. Garbage trucks weaved around parked cars, attempting to clean up the messes that had been piled at everyone's curbside. A few months had passed since the hurricane, but the wound felt fresh.

Earlier that day, Alice likened her experience to a dream from which she still had not awakened. Such disasters happened to other people, but not to her, she said. There, standing in the middle of her water-soaked first floor after she was allowed to return to her neighborhood and check in on her home, she broke down. Alice didn't want to cry in front of her husband. They had been together so long, and she knew it would upset him—but she had reached a breaking point. The bottled-up emotion washed over her as tears slowly dripped down her cheeks. Alice kept wondering how they would ever come back from this. And who would help them? She talked about this dread:

> I felt overwhelmed thinking about all the work that needed to be done in order to fix everything. I also knew we didn't have a lot of options. Somehow, someway we needed to get out from under this enormous weight and return to where we were—comfortable, happy, and enjoying our later years in life after thirty good years of marriage.

After a full day in Houston spent driving around and talking with service providers, survivors, and administrators, we grasped how this would be a project unlike any we had ever researched—and that it would be more difficult than we had imagined. We headed out of Houston and drove south to Pearland, one of the many smaller bedroom communities in the metro area that was particularly hard hit. Record rainfall had been recorded in Pearland. Their storm sewer system was overwhelmed, as well as their sanitary sewer system. Entire neighborhoods had been inundated with large amounts of water that transformed their small creeks into raging rivers.

Pearland school district employees and residents told us stories that differed from what we had heard closer to downtown Houston. We drove around some of the fringe communities and saw streets that had been broadcast on the national news. Trash piled ten or fifteen feet in the air sat, demanding removal. Every house on both sides of the streets had a curb full of furniture, clothing, household goods, and bags and bags of garbage that had been sitting there for weeks.

The obvious difference between these neighborhoods and the ones we saw earlier in the day was the quiet. As we drove around, we could hear the occasional dog barking and noise from the interstate, but those were the only sounds to break the eerie silence. No one milled about. No white dust coated the ground. No trucks worked in frenzied activity. This recovery was *very* different. Pearland was barely moving.

We tried to speak with some individuals and organizations in and around Pearland, but they were not in a position to spend much time with us to learn about our project's goals. These people were still in survival mode—now close to two months after the storm had hit. What we saw in Pearland began to set up a different narrative, one that contrasted the metropolitan areas with the small towns and cities dotting the Texas Gulf Coast.

Our first personal introduction to the recovery puzzle and the complexity of interviewing in a post-disaster setting happened the moment we walked into the Houston Community College shelter. Weaving through heavy traffic and congested side streets, not far from downtown, and passing by the arenas and stadiums that were an important part of the Houston story, we found this shelter had security like we had not encountered before. Once we were reluctantly let into the compound by Houston City police, we encountered another layer of security of Red Cross personnel outside the large warehouse shelter. After spending some time talking with them, we were finally allowed to go into the main shelter to try and meet up with our contact. The first person we encountered was our FEMA contact, with whom we had been communicating with for several weeks prior to arriving in Houston. This person, we thought, was going to help us establish our protocol for interviewing survivors in the shelters. When we arrived at the shelter in that early afternoon and went to the main door, we met Carlos, who warned us that this would not be as easy as he'd originally led us to believe. Though he was certainly willing to allow us to interview shelter residents, other people had responsibilities and leadership at the shelter—including the American Red Cross. Carlos and his FEMA colleagues had endured a rough week. The communication between team leaders from different organizations had been strained, and it seemed everyone was jockeying for a better position in order to leave Houston and move down to provide assistance in Florida (Hurricane Irma) and Puerto Rico (Hurricane Maria). The Red Cross was now our gatekeeper—and it looked like they were going to be the only way into this shelter and any of the others like it.

Rumors were floating around that this facility would be closing down by the end of the next week—so we needed to move fast. We had talked to the Red Cross on the ground in Houston the week before, and in conversations with their administrative team, we were led to believe that we could do the work as proposed, as long as we got there as soon as possible and were minimally invasive in the process.

We spent the next couple of hours trying to find the right person to give us clearance, and once we finally found her, she told us to talk to someone with more authority—someone at the Red Cross headquarters in Washington, DC—to receive permission to interview shelter residents. Even though we had engaged in multiple conversations about this project just a week before, we saw the landscape was quickly changing.

That afternoon, we never made it past the front door gathering space in the warehouse. Disappointed, we went back to the car to make some frantic phone calls to the national headquarters in Washington, DC. By close to 5:00 p.m. on the East Coast, our odds at resolving the issue were not looking good. We had planned to train interviewers and deploy them the following afternoon, and the one place we *thought* we were going to secure interviews was looking more and more like a no-go. What Carlos did not tell us at that time, but would later communicate to us through text and email, is that the Red Cross had been running the show at this location and all locations along the coast; they needed to shut the place down and move on. The shelter population was dwindling, and once these people left the shelter, we would lose a concentrated opportunity to talk with them about their experiences at the shelter and their plans for long-term recovery.

This part of the story did not end well for us. We would eventually be denied entry by everyone up the command ladder at the Red Cross. They were protecting the confidentiality of the citizens and felt that any interviewing at this time would be disruptive. Even though we carefully described our intentions, explained who was funding the project, outlined the type of information we were collecting, and argued for why understanding this experience from the survivors' perspective was important, the Red Cross did not seem to care. Our prior conversations no longer mattered. We even went as far as to contact our Arkansas congressmen to see if their staff could broker some type of mutually beneficial arrangement—but the Red Cross headquarters still said no. Did they really not want people talking to others about their experience? Did they not want people to find out about life in their shelters? As we found out later, the people of the Texas Gulf Coast had a lot to say about the Red Cross and FEMA. And it was certainly not all positive.

It Seems Complicated

Interviewing survivors in a disaster zone was like navigating murky waters, but we still wanted to know the stories behind the complicated response and recovery process. Specifically, we anticipated that people would adapt and function differently during the disaster process, and we were already witnessing this firsthand. As such, we expected to find that this mode of adaptation would significantly impact a survivor's social capital and resources. Worst-case scenario, the impact on those social networks and capital would be significant enough to impede the post-disaster adjustment among survivors. Trying to find as diverse a pool of survivors with varying experiences, and living in different locations along the coast, was key to assessing these expectations.

The pathway for individual recovery varies a great deal across subpopulation, location, type of disaster, etc. Not long after we deployed our interviewers, a news report came out that provided a glimpse of what had been happening months after the disaster and how disproportionately the storm's impact had been felt across the region. Based on survey results from a Kaiser Family Foundation and Episcopal Health Foundation study that interviewed over 1,600 Hurricane Harvey survivors all along the Texas Gulf Coast, recovery appeared to be moving slowly and had impacted places and persons very differently.[2]

We will discuss this well-executed survey in more detail in the pages that follow. The Kaiser Family Foundation graciously provided us with their data to help us tell what we hope is a more complete story of response and recovery. They also provided a summary of their findings, which concluded that nearly 50 percent of their respondents were still dealing, on a daily basis, with some type of post-disaster disruption. The same interviewees sensed that their communities were at risk for failure, and nearly two-thirds of the 1,660+ respondents still thought a lack of resources was the most important piece missing in their recovery puzzle.

Political scientist Daniel Aldrich presents a well-crafted discussion of the role that community plays during and after natural disasters in his book *Building Resilience: Social Capital in Post-Disaster Recovery*. Aldrich provides important insights into community capacity and the role of resilience in determining whether or not communities bounce back, and if so, the critical ingredients that make up the formula for success.[3] Recovery is not just about residents returning after a disaster. Aldrich characterizes it as a complex configuration of sociodemographic shifts, housing construction, population change, and access to sustained, comprehensive aid. There is no mystery as to why respondents to the Kaiser Foundation survey felt like they were still in recovery; they were, they are, and they will be for some time.

After Hurricane Katrina pummeled New Orleans and the Mississippi Gulf Coast, the popular press kept asking, "When will the people of New Orleans return home?" What the media didn't realize, and what many post-disaster assessments often ignore, is that recovery for some looks longer, more complicated, and more expensive. To move back to the Garden District in New Orleans was a different process than moving back to the Ninth Ward. Hurricane Harvey survivors were faced with similar hurdles that varied depending on the nexus of place, class, and race. In this regard, Harvey has not been any different from the last twenty natural disasters that struck cities and towns across America.

As we mentioned earlier, in addition to the interview data that we gathered, we were given access to the data from the Kaiser Family Foundation project that collected detailed information from residents on the Texas Gulf Coast who were recovering from Hurricane Harvey. This data added a layer of depth and breadth to our work; 1,600 additional voices describing their experiences and current post-disaster recovery circumstances seemed like it was almost too good to be true. Social scientists often struggle to get a random, representative sample with valid and reliable responses, and we do not take the Kaiser data for granted.

Part of our goal has been to give as much voice to residents living in different areas along the coast as possible. The majority of interviews had to take place in the larger metro areas, but we did not want to make this a story about the city alone. The Kaiser Family Foundation data helped us to tell a more nuanced story; and when the foundation returned to the Texas Gulf Coast a year after Hurricane Harvey had struck to ask more pointed questions about recovery, their work helped us even more. Their second round of research interviews addressed survivors a year post-Harvey to see how they were adjusting to a "new normal."

So, armed with personal interviews and online survey responses, we looked to cast a wide net, soliciting feedback from survivors about personal experiences, circumstances, attitudes, beliefs, and emotions. Recovery is about more than how people feel, though feelings are certainly part of it. For our purposes, it was also where people were, how they evacuated, and where they are right now. It's a personal story, but also a story about communities, families, places of work, centers of worship, and neighbors. Our big questions tackled the survivors' mental and physical health, attitudes about recovery and the future, family background and history, work history, and social relationships. We wanted to know where people looked for support, how big their social support network was, how they viewed this support network, and what constituted their social capital. Was it mostly homophilous, representing some version of bonding social capital, or was it more diverse and heterogeneous with the promise of the development of bridging and linking social capital? We will dive deeper into these forms of social capital later. Regardless, ours were not exclusively single-response questions. Unlike the majority of the Kaiser Foundation Family survey responses, our interviews were comprehensive, requiring detailed responses and often more than simple yes-or-no answers. But before we peel back the layers of responses, we want to provide some background on the respondents as well as some specifics regarding the comprehensive data collected by the Kaiser Family Foundation.

We made a decision early on in the data-gathering process to try some new approaches. Typically by now—nearly two years after collecting the data we're presenting here—we would have already churned through our quantitative data and written up the results for a series of articles to send to professional journals in public health, sociology, communication, etc. However, we discovered early in the project that in order to tell a story, to listen carefully to the survivors, and to do more than just record another uneven natural disaster, we would need to adapt our process.

We decided that a storytelling/narrative approach would let us lean in and listen to people's words when appropriate. At the same time, we needed the comprehensive data we collected to illuminate the circumstances and problems described by a population that doesn't always have the opportunity to tell their stories. We may hear a story on the news, or read about a family that tragically lost everything in the newspaper, but we wanted to provide a cross-section of these experiences. Not everyone was impacted equally, so the storyline had to be more than one thread. A face-to-face, semi-structured interview format would allow interviewers to navigate respondents through a set of prepared topics, but interviewees would have the opportunity to embellish their responses at will. We also interviewed people online with the same set of questions, but via this method, survivors could write their responses in private. Most importantly, after the primary data collection was completed, we were able to secure interviews/narratives from nearly forty people with open-ended conversations that provided context, stories, photographs, and insights well beyond what we might have received from a prescribed list of questions. These narratives yielded a rich and deeply personal account of what happened before, during, and after the storm.

Who Were Our Respondents?

Our respondents' social, demographic, and circumstantial contexts are useful for framing the more detailed information we collected. Of the 316 interviews conducted (both online and in-person), the vast majority (65 percent) lived in and around the Houston metropolitan area at the time of the storm.

Our respondents were scattered all over the city. The majority owned their own homes, and 40 percent were renters. Renting an apartment, mobile home, or some other structure and facing the devastation of Hurricane Harvey clearly meant something different from those persons facing damage to the structures they owned.

The large majority of people we interviewed reported being interested in returning to their residence. However, a number of renters were not convinced that their apartments or rentals would be ready anytime soon. Even if those apartments were made available, renters doubted whether the repairs and/or improvements would be made in a timely fashion or with the necessary care to convince them that going back to those places would be the right decision. Renters assumed that if landlords left their apartments in poor condition *before* the storm, they would certainly fail to improve them *after* the storm. Some people had lived in flood-prone areas and now expressed a refusal to live in one again. A low inventory of affordable housing severely limited survivors' options; still others had no place to return to.

As expected, homeowners had a different perspective. The majority whose homes were not totally destroyed were interested in returning and rebuilding/repairing their residences. For them, a home was more than a building; it was often an important part of their roots and family history. Their children attended the neighborhood schools, their friends lived close by, and their work was within a reasonable driving distance. Many survivors remarked how convenient their neighborhood was to the amenities that brought them to that location in the first place. One homeowner that we spoke with when driving through Alice's neighborhood in early October remarked, "Our family lived here long enough that even if we came back to a shell of a house, we had already decided we were going to fix it up into the home it had been no matter how long it took."

We found it interesting how many homeowners relied on words like *neighborhood, community, family, location,* and *friends* to characterize the reasons for returning to a damaged home. Physical place was important for these homeowners, but so was their social capital—their connections, support, and community engagement. Of those respondents who owned their residences, over 70 percent said the people living in the neighborhood would likely help one another as opposed to going their own way. More than one-third of those residents said they talked with their neighbors every day; half reported doing something together in the last year that was seen as an improvement to the neighborhood. Many of these people were connected, and their recovery stories differed from the stories of survivors who were isolated, lacked social capital, and lacked a social support safety net, such as critical necessities for relief and recovery in the absence of friends and relatives.

We made every effort to interview a diverse group of survivors, so the sociodemographic profile of our interviewees reflects the diversity of the general population composition in the coastal areas impacted by this natural disaster. The racial breakdown in the interviewees was approximately 71 percent white and 29 percent nonwhite; the majority of nonwhite respondents were African American, and about 29 percent (either white or nonwhite) self-reported their Hispanic origin. At this point, it is worth mentioning that throughout this book, nonwhite individuals include people who identify as Black/African American/Afro Caribbean, Asian, Native American, or multiracial. While we understand that the lived experience of each racial category is by no means homogeneous, for the purposes of our data analysis, we broke race into two categories.

Furthermore, the gender split was relatively even, and the median age of interviewees was thirty-eight years of age. The majority of residents with whom we talked had at least one child under the age of seventeen, and 20 percent of households had more than three children present at the time of the storm. Nearly one-third of the interviewees had a high school education or less, but the overwhelming majority (70+ percent) had some advanced education beyond high school.

Finally, this group of interviewees had a pretty diverse work history. Sixty percent reported working before Hurricane Harvey made landfall, and the vast majority (80 percent) had full-time jobs where they had been working for an average of 3.5 years. A number of employed respondents reported that their place of work was significantly impacted by the storm, and about half of those employed said their workplace was flooded, inaccessible, or in need of repair. Many survivors were self-employed and had lost their "home base" of operation, which jeopardized their work. Alice was one of those self-employed storm survivors. She had not been able to respond to the work demand between scheduling visits to her lawyer's offices and maintaining her husband's failing health—all while struggling to find a temporary place to live and worrying about repairs to her home.

Alice's Story Continues

We wanted to check in on Alice, so we called her nearly five months after we first talked with her in early October. She and her husband had still not moved back into their home and were patiently waiting on repairs to be completed. After moving out of the La Quinta, they now had a one-bedroom apartment. Their lawsuit against the city was still active in the courts and didn't seem to be moving along, and Alice had taken a leave of absence from work with the promise of returning once things got back to "normal." She talked for ten minutes as she drove across town, and we did not sense much hope in her voice. There was much that still needed to be done. She didn't mention receiving help from anyone or any organization that could have helped her navigate the messiness. She'd had what she described as a perfect life before the storm, but here she was, five months later, living in a one-bedroom apartment, thirty minutes from her damaged home, with her husband's health declining, her work in limbo, and her social network in shambles.

Nothing in our data, and nothing from our extended conversations with survivors, indicates that stories like Alice's are unique. Now here we are in 2019, and stories are still coming out of Houston. Months after the storm, life in the fourth largest city in America was far from normal. A February 2018 AP wire story noted that more than three thousand households were still living in hotels, and thousands more were living in their homes and apartments awaiting repairs. Mayor Sylvester Turner said, "While we acknowledge that we are making progress, we also want to be very clear the recovery is not happening fast enough for any of us."[4] The article estimated that Houston faces over 2.5 billion dollars in repairs to city infrastructure and buildings that could take years to complete. Academic research is trickling in identifying circumstances that are concerning and pointing to a structured inequality that has unequally affected lower-income, minority populations post-disaster.[5]

Alice's recovery process drags on. She waits on contractors, waits on federal and state assistance, waits on the courts to make a decision . . . and she continues to wait. Why can't we do better for people like Alice? Why does recovery after a natural disaster like Harvey have to drag on for months and years? Do we think we are better prepared or equipped than we actually are? Is there that much of a disconnect between individuals and the communities that makes recovery more difficult than it needs to be? How does this disconnect impact recovery, and is it the same for everyone? Unfortunately, we don't know the answers to all of these questions, particularly as they apply to Hurricane Harvey survivors. Nevertheless, we are hopeful that in the pages that follow, readers can begin to understand a little more about the grief that is tied to recovery and the types of community programming that, if implemented, could lead to successful long-term recovery and resilience-building for the next natural disaster awaiting the Texas Gulf Coast and beyond.

3

Every Picture Tells a Story

When natural disasters strike photographers stand at the ready to capture the perfect, unforgettable image that becomes seared into our memory forever. Before smartphones were part of everyday life, *Life, Time, Newsweek, U.S. News & World Report, National Geographic,* and every other print news outlet relied on award-winning photographers to tell the natural disaster story. Consider the indelible image of the widow standing in the middle of her house the morning after it was torn from its foundation by an EF 4 tornado. Or the people jammed shoulder to shoulder, waiting to board one of the "Cajun Navy" boats that had lined up to rescue Katrina's flood victims. Or the darkened side streets in downtown San Juan, Puerto Rico, weeks after Hurricane Maria cut a swath of destruction through the island.

Such pictures have been plastered all over social media, newspapers, magazines, and the evening news. And now, with the advent of the smartphone, almost anyone has the potential to be a citizen-journalist and capture images that communicate to the world what disaster looks like. Personal social media posts, off-center photographs, blurry images, and choppy videos have changed the way we communicate and the way we have come to understand tragedy and disaster recovery—all because the survivors can now document the events.

Of course, photographs only capture a fraction of the emotion and hurt that accompanies disaster. Sometimes the loss is so overwhelming that survivors struggle to put that enormity into words. Others find it cathartic to talk about the loss. It certainly seemed that way for Linda, who was forthcoming with stories and even sent pictures she had taken throughout the storm and its aftermath. On the phone, months after her first interview, she recounted her disaster experiences and then described some particularly meaningful and poignant pictures.

She told us that after Harvey made landfall and the water started to rise at her apartment complex, her family hurried to grab a few items and evacuate. The kids took their favorite toys, and she packed a few clothes and stuffed them into big, black garbage bags. She described the boats rescuing people all over the apartment complex as daylight faded. Some even used air mattresses as floats to carry along their belongings. When she and her kids finally got into a boat, they did not have room for anything else. Darkness fell as her sister and her brother-in-law waited at the end of the neighborhood street where the water was lower. Most of the electricity was shut off in the area. It was quiet, and she sensed her kids were scared. "We loaded everything we had into my sister's husband's truck and drove back to their apartment," she said. "It seemed like we would never get there. Roads were closed; there were lots of detours, and lots of traffic with people trying to get away from the rising water. It took us more than an hour to travel about ten miles just south of Houston. I knew it was going to be bad when I came back to it. I just didn't think it would be this bad."[1]

As Linda described the pictures she had sent us, Figure 3.1 seemed to capture the feeling of loss and desperation she and her family felt post-Harvey. Almost a week after the water receded, she had taken a picture of the inside of her apartment. Police and city officials had finally let the residents return home to check on things and salvage whatever they could. It was hot that morning, and she and her sister sat in disbelief outside the apartment, drenched in sweat after spending hours rummaging around for something that was not wet, moldy, or destroyed. By the looks of things, they didn't have much luck. Linda said she just started piling things in the living room to drag out to the curb. The loss she felt wasn't monetary in that moment, but sentimental—baby photos, pictures of her parents, the kids' schoolwork that she had saved. She was glad her children didn't have to be there to see this mess, to be filled with disappointment and sadness at what they would never be able to replace.

Right before the storm, Linda had bought a bike for her middle child. He begged for it all summer, and she had finally promised to buy one for him once school started back up again. This was not an easy purchase for Linda. Bills, loans, and food were priority expenses, and after taking care of those necessities, not much money was left over. But her son insisted. Every boy his age in the apartment complex had a bike, she recalled, and she knew how bad he wanted it.

Figure 3.1. Apartment Cleanup. Credit: Linda (pseudonym)

When the water came, Linda didn't have time to grab the bike. Her son cried about wanting to look for it, but the water had already risen above Linda's knees. Her picture, Figure 3.2, captures what she and her family came back to: a flood-ravaged home, and the bike. It needed a new chain and a few other parts—another expense that Linda and her family could not afford. When she described this picture, she said it reminded her of how helpless she'd felt upon evacuating—how unprepared she was, and how devastated she felt to leave behind irreplaceable things.

We want to unpack these images by using survivors' words to complement the photographs they took. When survivors rely upon a photograph to express a thought or feeling, these pictures become disaster artifacts: representations of a moment or circumstance that contribute to the narrative of displacement and destruction while epitomizing sensations that are hard to describe with language. In addition to photographs, other materials, such as maps and diagrams, charts, and tables, tell another part of the complicated natural disaster story. This combination represents part reflection and part documentation, and we provide these other visuals to offer insight beyond words.

Figure 3.2. Muddied Bicycle. Credit: Linda (pseudonym)

We have combined all of these sources—photographs, research visuals, our interviews, and the Kaiser Family Foundation interviews—to provide deeper glimpses into the stories and circumstances of the disaster. We hope to triangulate the data in a meaningful manner that offers a multidimensional look at an event that demands our scrutiny, and to bring voice to those whose lives were most impacted by Hurricane Harvey.

Displacement

As seen in Table 3.1, slightly more than half of the persons we interviewed were displaced and sought refuge in a traditional shelter that was run by the Red Cross, Salvation Army, or another disaster relief organization. The majority of shelters were closed by the time we deployed our interviewers in October 2017, and by then most of the survivors had scattered all over southeastern Texas. Some found refuge in hotels in Houston and other major cities. Others left those hotels and went elsewhere to stay with friends or relatives that were outside of the disaster zone. Newspaper reports described anguish and thinned patience. Neighborhoods were trying to recover fully—both physically and emotionally—and some of those residents were going to have to think long and hard whether or not that would be the best plan for them moving forward.[2]

Not surprisingly, most survivors said nothing good about being displaced (Table 3.2). Those who took up residence in a hotel or motel were collectively the most satisfied group, whereas more than 75 percent of respondents who had taken refuge in a shelter were very dissatisfied. This group had twice as many respondents expressing high levels of dissatisfaction than those fortunate enough to be in a hotel or motel. What happened to everyone when the disaster relief shelters closed? Did they head to hotels/motels? We know that in Houston, some shelter-dwellers were homeless before the storm, and some of them went back to being homeless or went to the Salvation Army or New Hope housing. This marginally housed population was the most threatened, and many of them lost everything but the clothes on their backs as well as the odds and ends they had stuffed into backpacks as the water rose. During our first visit in October, one of the New Hope Housing residents described his circumstance to us in those early hours and days of the storm. "Man, I was lucky to get out of where I was staying," he said. "It just seemed like the water came out of nowhere and before I could gather much, everything was already wet. Me and a couple of my buddies wandered around for a few days."

He described his continued uncertainty and the fear he felt staying several nights in an old abandoned building. But the scene there, as he described it, was not good. He noted drugs, drinking, and fighting, and all he wanted was to find a quiet and safe place to sleep. He knew that he had to get out of there and eventually, a shelter opened close to where

TABLE 3.1. Displacement Outcomes

Hotel/Motel 13%

Shelter 51%

Friends/Family 36%

TABLE 3.2. Satisfaction with Displacement Outcomes

	Very Satisfied	Satisfied	Dissatisfied	Very Dissatisfied
Friend/Relative	9.1%	18.2%	45.5%	27.3%
Hotel/Motel	21.4%	7.1%	57.1%	13.3%
Shelter	15.6%	9.4%	39.1%	35.9%

Figure 3.3. Houston Community College Warehouse Shelter.
Credit: Kevin M. Fitzpatrick

he and his friends were staying near the baseball stadium. He described a big FEMA and Red Cross warehouse and a "sea of volunteers." It took them several hours to process him, but he was finally assigned a bed in what became a pretty noisy and crowded space. Sure, this new shelter was safe and dry—but he had no idea how long he would be able to last there. The air conditioning struggled to cool such a big space. After the first couple of weeks, he said, people were on edge.

After talking with him and others, we got the impression that no one really wanted to be in the temporary shelters. But they had nowhere else to go. Our anonymous respondent was homeless before the storm, and he would likely be homeless unless he could find a spot in a shelter or get on a list for supportive housing. He went on to say,

> Man, there were women and their kids separated in the space from everyone else but it was still in the open. Kids screaming, running around, throwing up, coughing, sneezing—it was like a hospital waiting room. I heard they would be making additional space at several other shelters—I couldn't wait to get out.[3]

In many ways, this resident's story of the trials and tribulations of staying in a shelter confirms much of what we had learned from conversations with other survivors. Noise was a common complaint, and over 40 percent of those relegated to temporary shelters felt the way other people acted—as highlighted by this survivor's recollection of drug use, drinking, and fighting—was a problem.

We took the photo in Figure 3.3 on our first day in Houston, but it only tells part of the story. When we visited this shelter in the early part of October, we learned of a major push all along the impacted Texas Gulf Coast to close down the large warehouse shelters. These shelters were expensive to run, and because of the busy hurricane season, manpower and resources were being diverted to Florida and Puerto Rico. On the day we visited the Houston Community College warehouse shelter, people were starting to move out. The City of Houston was offering six months of free housing to persons currently in shelters as a stopgap strategy for moving people out as quickly as possible and closing down the shelters. Houston made apartments available with reduced/free utilities and rent; all residents had to do was sign a six-month lease before being transported to a fully furnished location. Sounds good? Maybe at first, but what would the city do once the six-month temporary leases were up?

Damage and Disruption

While some residents were lucky enough to have experienced no damage as a result of the storm (25 percent), the vast majority of our respondents reported mild to total destruction. Nearly half (43 percent) were either not sure if they would return to their original residences or had already decided not to return. Many said they could not handle living through another version of Harvey. Others knew their homes were contaminated and lost—and that it did not make sense to return to a place not worth salvaging.

Survivors who rented their dwellings were less committed to their homes and said they most likely would not return to them. This is a troubling finding. Given the role that emotional investment in the physical community plays in an individual's likelihood to stay and help rehabilitate the area,[4] we couldn't help but wonder if this reluctance was an ominous sign for the resilience of the Texas Gulf Coast. In fact, a recent news report suggests that some long-established neighborhoods in Port Arthur will not rebuild. Residents have not returned, and reports now

Table 3.3. How Much Disruption?	
Very Disrupted	12%
Still Disrupted	20%
Almost Normal	25%
Back to Normal	40%

claim the population of Port Arthur has declined by nearly five thousand people. Such a decline could cause major problems for that city moving forward, particularly with respect to their eligibility for receiving federal funds.[5] The people we interviewed from smaller places were often more compelled to return compared to those living in larger cities, likely because the options were limited in these smaller locales than in Houston or Galveston.

The story of disruption was not all that different when we examined the Kaiser Family Foundation responses seen in Table 3.3. Similar to the survivors we interviewed, a large number of Kaiser Family Foundation respondents reported mild damage to total destruction (43 percent). But even after three long months of recovery, they were still struggling with the chaos.

More than half of the survivors interviewed by the Kaiser Family Foundation continued to experience disruption post-Harvey.[6] For some, the biggest challenge of the recovery process was finding contractors to do home repairs or waiting for them to schedule the work they had promised to complete months ago. These survivors also continued to feel the financial impact of Hurricane Harvey. The survivors lost wages and exhausted resources, including money that had been put away for retirement, college funds, and emergencies. Some struggled to pay their bills, and others faced imminent bankruptcy and the fear of starting all over again.

Capturing Race and Place Differences

Given the prior research examining the details and complexity of natural disaster impact, coupled with news coming out of Houston and the rest of the Texas Gulf Coast, we hypothesized that the storm experience and recovery process for this region would differ from group to group and place to place. Fear, tragedy, and loss would dominate the narratives, but considerable variations would also emerge—especially regarding the places they lived and their sociodemographic and economic backgrounds.

The data from our interviews reflects this consensus. Significant differences existed between white and nonwhite survivors regarding their chosen path of displacement. (See Table 3.4.) An overwhelming majority of nonwhite interviewees used traditional shelter options post-disaster, while the majority of white interviewees relied on friends and family to shelter them when Hurricane Harvey hit the coast.

Not surprisingly, the Kaiser Family Foundation reported significant differences between racial and ethnic groups on a number of different factors related to experiences and circumstances during and after Hurricane Harvey. One significant difference between racial and ethnic groups was how they reported damage to their apartment/house due to Hurricane Harvey. (See Table 3.5.) Black residents in particular had significantly higher reports of damage to their house or apartment than any other group—nearly 15 percent higher than the average resident who was interviewed.

Income data amplified these differences. Survivors who reported lower income levels (100 percent below the federal poverty level) were nearly twice as likely to report damage to their homes or apartments compared to those who reported higher income levels. This was also the

Table 3.4. Percent Displacement Path by Race and Ethnicity

	Hispanic	White	Nonwhite
Shelter/Homeless	50%	38%	71%
Hotel/Motel	15%	13%	12%
Friend/Relative	35%	49%	17%

Table 3.5. Percent Reporting Damage by Race and Ethnicity

White	38%
Black	55%
Hispanic	45%
Total Residents	43%

case for persons interviewed by the Kaiser Family Foundation; persons at the lowest income levels were less likely to have flood insurance compared to their higher income counterparts. Other income group comparisons made in the Kaiser Family Foundation report tell an important part of the natural disaster story and reinforce what we have come to know about natural disasters in the United States and around the world: that survivors are not all equal when it comes to how they are impacted during a storm and how they experience the rebuilding and recovery process.[7]

Some places escaped the massive devastation that many Texas Gulf Coast residents saw with Hurricane Harvey. What did that mean, and how different were those experiences? Harvey was a storm like none other that had hit the region, and FEMA's image gives us a pretty good idea of the extent of damage, as well as the pattern of damage. Certain communities escaped with only minor work to be done, while others are still trying to put the pieces back together.

Looking at this map (Figure 3.4), there is a clear connection between the more damaged areas and the locations where we did the majority of our interviewing. Harris, Jefferson, Brazoria, and Nueces Counties—where we conducted most of our interviews—also reported the largest number of individual assistance applications. But upon listening to survivors tell their stories and looking at various disaster responses across the counties, we determined that not everyone's experience was the same. In other words, the map only tells part of the story.

By the time we arrived at the Gulf Coast in October 2017 (nearly two months after the storm), the garbage piles told a story of their own. For instance, in some neighborhoods we visited in Houston, residents were ready to rebuild: everything was stripped down to the studs, and progress was underway. As we drove by the house shown in Figure 3.5, the homeowner and builder were in the middle of finalizing reconstruction plans. Our conversation with them left us thinking that this situation was probably an anomaly. The man told us that they had pretty much lost everything, but that the salvage operation on their neighborhood's houses had been going nonstop since the contractors were allowed back in. His family went back and forth about whether rebuilding was even worthwhile, but they were so sideways on their mortgage (plus other debts) that they needed the insurance settlement and whatever

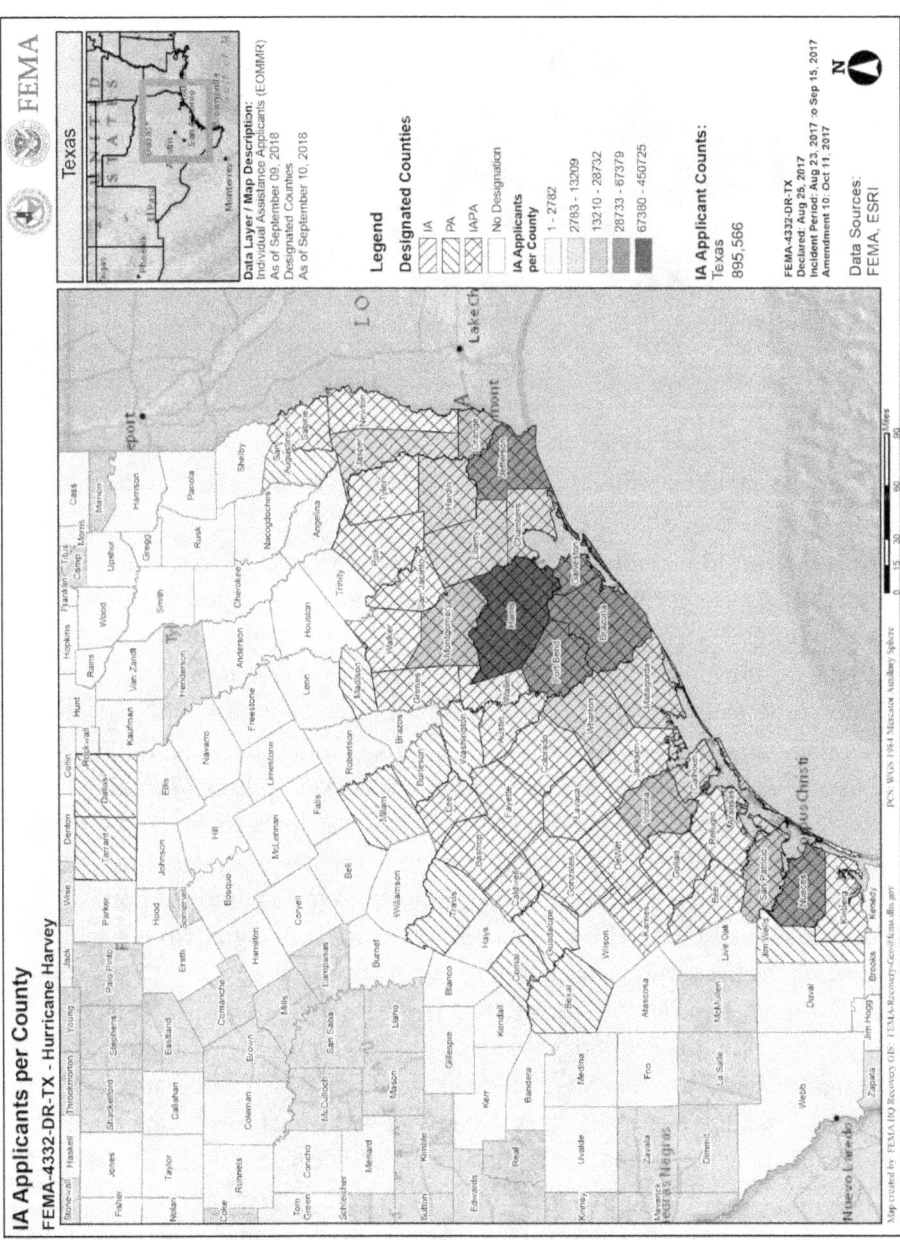

Figure 3.4. Disaster Assistance (FEMA) Applications for Texas Counties. Credit: U.S. Department of Homeland Security, FEMA

Figure 3.5. House Stripped to the Studs. Credit: Kevin M. Fitzpatrick

tiny amount of federal assistance they would receive. He reminded us that his hands were tied, and "[rebuilding] was pretty much all that we could do."[8]

As we moved further down the coast out of Houston proper and into some of the neighborhoods on the outer boundaries of Harris County, the story shifted. No one was talking much about rebuilding. No one was hauling off garbage. No one was even milling around, let alone any contractors. Our drive along highways, down streets, and into small communities provided glimpses into the devastating stories we collected—but the silence at times was deafening. Abandoned homes. Garbage piled high, with no promise of removal in sight. No electric saws or the background sounds of hammering.

Survivors told varying stories about the recovery process. Marta managed to escape the brunt of the storm, but this was not the case for her daughter's family. While Marta and her family sustained moderate damage and had their own struggles to contend with, what was taking place with her daughter Katie's family consumed her. She recounted how heartbreaking it was to drive up and down the streets and see everyone's belongings on the curb. The smell was horrible. To her knowledge the Red Cross and other large organizations had done nothing at the time in their neighborhood. Most of the help Marta and her family received was from the Salvation Army—whom they described as "God's blessing"—but the main recovery efforts they witnessed were neighbors helping neighbors.[9]

Marta's story exemplifies the problem of getting aid to smaller towns—an element of recovery thematic to the survivors' stories. Rural residents were the last to receive aid, and they felt abandoned. Some responders argued that recovery organizations like the Red Cross and FEMA were problematic in terms of where they were and were not in the weeks and months that followed.

Marta was unhappy with FEMA. She found their behavior shameful—giving people hope and then denying them assistance. The cruelty for Marta lay in how FEMA sent down workers—people whom she described as "making big salaries"—into small, rural communities to take down survivors' information, only to deny them assistance. Marta's daughter and her family were denied assistance and had no place to live, or put their pets. They ended up moving in with Marta and her husband in already cramped quarters because of the ongoing repairs being made on their home. For Marta, FEMA was a national disgrace that cared little about what was going on in her tiny community.

Marta further expressed a general sense of malaise—again, because of what her daughter faced. Katie was able to salvage a few clothes and

Figure 3.6a–b. Pearland Homes. Credit: Kevin M. Fitzpatrick

household items, but nothing more. What remained she put into large black plastic bags and stored them in the garage to wait. For weeks, Marta said, she and her daughter sifted through clothes and ran load after load of laundry. The local dry cleaners also pitched in, working overtime for the community and cleaning clothes for free. It was an emotional time for Marta and her daughter as they sifted through years of memories from her daughter's childhood—things she'd taken with her when she gotten married and started her own family. Altogether they managed to collect, clean, and keep ten plastic tubs full of clothing, memories, and important documents. Marta said she and her daughter expressed many emotions and shed many tears during that time, and though they grew closer while working together, they both stayed angry. They felt the government was not doing their part, and the women mourned the assistance they would never receive. She finished talking with us and left us with a powerful rhetorical question: "Where did all that money go that was donated to the Red Cross? I can assure you, no one in this town received any of it."

Many of the people we interviewed sounded a lot like Marta. Later on, we discuss at length how citizens assisted each other during recovery efforts, and many of our interviewees spoke as if this was the only help they received. Like Marta, they felt abandoned by the organizations and authorities and were grateful for the assistance of peers. The most comprehensive recovery efforts were concentrated in higher density communities—but so many more along the coast were impacted. In short, cleanup in Harris County (Houston) seemed to go a whole lot faster than cleanup in Refugio County (Port Aransas).

As we've mentioned, survivors were also willing to share the photographs they had taken since before the storm. The smartphone's ubiquity is important for a couple of reasons. First, people could document their own tragedy in real time. And second, people could document the level of destruction in detail—an important step for insurance claim purposes. No one with a smartphone needed to wait weeks and months for a claims adjuster to come all the way out to their property (though many survivors in the coastal towns of Texas did have to wait). Instead, survivors could take the photos, send them in to their insurance claims adjuster, and have a check mailed out to them in weeks. While that was probably the outcome for only a minority of claims

Figure 3.7a–b. Corpus Christi Neighborhood. Credit: Jack (pseudonym)

being settled along the coast, we know from listening to survivors who rebuilt fairly quickly that the insurance payments played a big part in that speed. Of course, those without insurance could not even make a claim at all.

For whatever reason, people took pictures and sent them to us. We could never be able to put them all in this book, but we wanted to present some of these images in order to add another layer to the survivors' stories. Further down the coast toward Corpus Christi, Jack sent pictures to us along with some description. The raw, unedited images (Figure 3.7a–b) of destruction in his rural neighborhood depicted the result of both the hurricane and the tornado that touched down on the backside of the storm. Houses were destroyed, and debris from trees, houses, and yards created a challenge for those cleaning up.

And Then What Happens?

The trajectory of recovery following natural disasters is not a straight path, but rather a set of peaks and valleys. The vacillating nature of disaster recovery is best visualized in DeWolfe's four phases of disaster: heroic, honeymoon, disillusionment, and reconstruction.[10]

In the spirit of this chapter, we wanted to use Figure 3.8 to help the reader better understand how residents experienced Hurricane Harvey compared to the practitioner and scholarly understanding of disaster recovery. As reflected in the figure, through the uptick in the heroic and honeymoon phases, emotional support in the community can be high. After facing a near-death experience, individuals feel a sense of relief having simply survived the disaster. The mood is defined by an overall sense of altruism that we will describe later on; as one survivor put it, "Recovery was all about neighbors helping neighbors." Residents often believe that if they can weather this storm and maintain

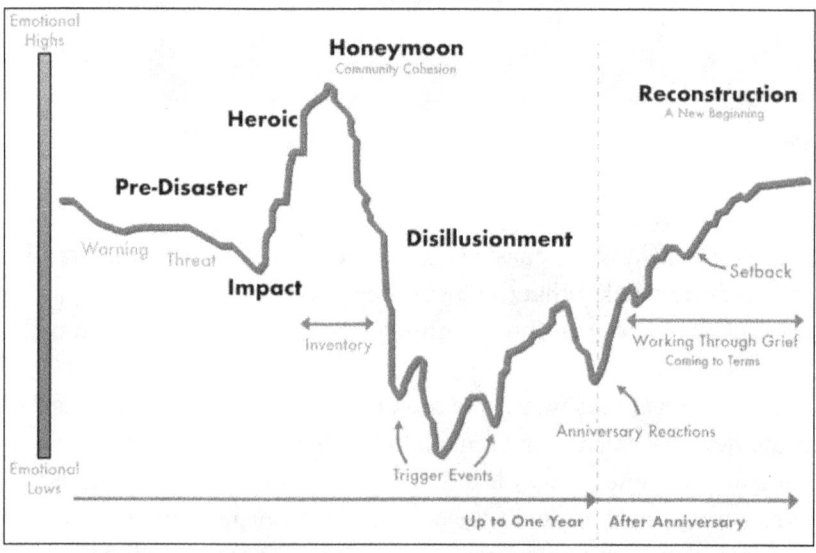

Figure 3.8. DeWolfe's Four Phases of Disaster. Adapted from Zunin & Myers as cited in DeWolfe, D. J. 2000. *Training Manual for Mental Health and Human Service Workers in Major Disasters.* 2nd ed. HHS Publication No. ADM 90–538. Rockville, MD: US Department of Health and Human Services, Substance Abuse and Mental Health Services Administration, Center for Mental Health Services.

their sense of community cohesion, they will find a way to recover and rebuild.

During the heroic and honeymoon phases, communities also experience an outpouring of media attention. Not long after Hurricane Harvey blew out to sea, images, videos, interviews, and stories flooded social media, the local and national news, and other outlets interested in telling stories about Harvey and its survivors. But the Harvey news cycle eventually slowed. As the media shifted its attention to other stories, the national focus did too. In this case, attention shifted to Florida and Puerto Rico. While this was understandable, Harvey became a tragedy within the tragedy—Harvey survivors ended up feeling like they had to fend for themselves.

Thus, the Texas Gulf Coast moved into the disillusionment phase fairly quickly, as the peaks of the heroic and honeymoon phase morphed into valleys. The disillusionment period is marked by a sense of the reality that awaits. Survivors know they still need help, but the bulk of support is no longer readily available. In Texas, the government and the Red Cross moved on, leaving only neighbors, churches, and local organizations to help.

Help Is on the Way

Interestingly, very few of the pictures sent to us featured any "official" organization in action. Mostly survivors captured images of neighbors, friends unaffected by the storm, local churches that rolled up their sleeves, and service providers who were undermanned and underprepared but ready to do what was necessary. In these moments, when the local community stepped in to fill the gap left by an absent media and thinly stretched federal agencies, the deep valleys of disillusionment began to slope upward as illustrated in the chart.

The recovery phase of this disaster was a massive human effort. People in fishing boats and canoes conducted individual rescues. One resident engineered a checklist to make sure that someone had made contact with everyone in her neighborhood (800-plus homes) and knew they were out of their houses and safe. Some individuals even planned and implemented neighborhood "stores," where residents could go to other people's homes and pick up cleaning supplies, food, and donated

Figure 3.9. Volunteer Staging. Credit: Jack (pseudonym)

clothing. Friends mucked out each other's houses when the water finally receded. Companies gave people volunteer days to help out others. The Mormon Church mobilized huge teams to dispose of the garbage in people's homes. Even kids cleaned out their neighbors' yards after all the big trash was removed. After more than a year post-storm, a Houston resident named Christine told us that the recovery effort carries on. "We continue to be involved in helping organize groups of volunteers to clean yards that are full of glass and debris. Social media groups are assisting with washing crews to help people who are finally moving back home."[11]

For some neighborhoods after Harvey, Figure 3.9 probably represented a welcome sight: household supplies, fresh water, bathrooms, and electricity—things we generally take for granted. Yet in many neighborhoods and towns along the coast, residents lacked necessities for days or even weeks. Christine's account reflected a common narrative: that the strength of neighborhoods was defined by the willingness of strangers to pitch in and help wherever necessary. While the *how* and *who* varied from place to place, a theme emerged. Over and over again, our respondents called attention to the citizen helpers and expressed heartfelt appreciation for the people who had helped them. For example, people from Louisiana with no material connection to the region brought a boat and drove around in neighborhoods, plucking people out of their houses and driving them to dry land. Churches from Alabama set up feeding stations and supply tents where people could get basic necessities. Local churches in Galveston, Houston, Pearland, Port Arthur, and all along the Texas Gulf Coast sent congregants to clean up, provide respite, and support their neighbors on the long, hard road to recovery.

Even though Diane had evacuated out of her Houston neighborhood early, her friend took this picture (Figure 3.10) from her front door as she was waiting for someone to rescue her and her family. Diane was financially advantaged compared to many of the people we interviewed, but nonetheless, her appreciation aligned with a common theme: she wanted to thank and praise those who assisted others during rescue and recovery.

She told us that it was difficult for her to request help. "How do you ask friends to take the risk that they need to come in and help you clean up a biohazard level 3 site (my house)?" she asked. Diane needed help with cleaning but also with salvaging whatever she could, so she asked her housecleaner, a friend, and her adult daughter to pitch in. No one expected payment, but Diane insisted on giving them something for spending several days assisting her. After cleaning and boxing up what she could, she told her contractor to start mucking out and repairing her house. From the start, her contractor was helpful and upbeat, and he assured her that everything would be okay, even though at the time she could not imagine moving back in at all. The idea of a totally reconditioned house free of mud, water, silt, mold, and horrible smells

Figure 3.10. High Water Rescue. Credit: Diane (pseudonym)

seemed like a dream—but Diane's contractor, her Harvey hero, made it a reality.

Diane is yet another respondent who described a rallying community. A group of affected and unaffected moms in the neighborhood sprang into action. These moms coordinated a rescue team with small boats and used social media to assist in the evacuation of those impacted in their neighborhood. One mom offered childcare before, during, and after the flooding—a service she is still providing. The moms in Diane's neighborhood also organized a get-together for the community to encourage everyone to share their stories, almost like an informal group therapy. Individuals offered services during these events—face-painting to cheer up the kids, book borrowing, meal sharing, and more. The moms organized the distribution of water, snacks, and meals, all made available at a neighborhood feeding station. They set up a Facebook group to help share information in real time, and families who had previously experienced floods could post information on what to do next, how FEMA works, how to deal with flood insurance adjusters, where to get supplies, how to find a contractor, etc.

All of the services she described carried on for several months and were "real sanity saver[s]," to use her words. The men got together and organized a security watch to cover all entrances to the neighborhood and worked with local and non-local law enforcement agencies to protect everyone's homes. This, combined with the active use of the Facebook group, gave everyone at least some peace of mind that they desperately needed. Diane felt the boost of support and claimed that it improved her mental health. She described how the unaffected families stripped out the damaged houses and sheltered, fed, and brought coffee and water to their neighbors. Many of them exposed themselves to what Diane described as "nasty pathogens, while spending hours in fetid water for us while we hugged one another and cried." Heroes had come alongside of them and helped them through this time of grief, asking for nothing in return. Again, local efforts made all the difference in Diane's life. Even now, more than a year later, she can reflect on just how important this was to her. Respondents overloaded us with details about the people who helped them and described their immense gratitude.

No Love Lost

When disasters occur, our natural reaction is to blame someone. "Someone did not get it right," we say. "Someone did not do his or her job. Someone dropped the ball." This inclination became apparent during our interviews, as people consistently expressed disappointment in FEMA, the Red Cross, and even their city governments. Most Americans believe these institutions are responsible for helping before, during, and after a natural disaster. However, there was no love lost as far as some of the survivors were concerned. Our respondents spoke at length about their dissatisfaction and disappointment with these organizations in particular—what they failed to do and what their lack of support and empathy meant to survivors. When asked directly what local, state, and national governments and agencies did to help in the recovery process, some of our respondents answered this way:

> The state was very slow to respond in the beginning. I think that when the state realized that we had become sitting ducks they seemed to move a little quicker. FEMA came in and drug [sic] their feet and had people feeling like they were going to be forgotten about. Red Cross was a joke; they had people jumping through hoops for $400. If it were not for my employer and my church I don't know what I would have done.[12]

> There was no help at the time that I know of from our state. Also, I was told there was help and people were getting it that didn't even experience any flooding. I heard all you had to do is wait in long lines and endure the weather outside for many hours. I was not able to do that, since I had to take my daughter to school and pick her up. Also, I was looking for a job in the meantime as well to help my girlfriend and also help with house repairs and clean up. So, I would describe our state's help as very questionable and not available to us.[13]

In response to questions from the Kaiser Family Foundation project about assistance from government and non-government agencies, over half of respondents reported that they felt they did not receive the assistance they needed.[14] More than 50 percent of African American respondents and persons living below the federal poverty level reported not getting needed support or assistance relative to their white or wealthier counterparts. The same discrepancy across racial and economic lines appeared when looking specifically at FEMA assistance. White and higher- and moderate-income applicants were more likely to receive assistance or be approved for assistance compared to lower-income minorities, particularly black residents. Of course, several mechanisms are crashing in at once on this process, and we are not implying an inherent bias exists in FEMA's application and awards system. Our intent is merely to report what the Kaiser Family Foundation found. However, this result does beg the question: Why does such a discrepancy exist across racial and economic lines? Here is what one person saw as the problem with the process when asked within a focus group setting run by the Kaiser Family Foundation:

> They came to my house and walked [around] my house and saw the damage. And they gave me $364.29. I know people who didn't have as much damage as I had that got thousands . . . I think it just all depends on the person that came to your house. The man that came to my house, he was like giving us real serious comments. He wasn't caring, and he wasn't very compassionate. He was in and out as fast as you could go. But I have a friend that had a lady and she was very nice. She came and walked through the house. She was compassionate. She didn't even have as much damage as I did and she got $2500.[15]

Not everyone had the same assessment. Some of the people that we interviewed gave their local and state governments high marks. Though local government, particularly the city of Houston, made significant decisions that impacted flooded neighborhoods, reviews were surprisingly positive. The majority of survivors interviewed by the Kaiser Family Foundation gave "excellent," "very good," or "good" evaluations of their governments in response to the Harvey disaster. The data in Table 3.6 are pretty clear. Governments received positive marks by the majority of respondents, and the further government was from the epicenter, the lower the marks. We examine this in more detail later in the book.

Whenever we encountered respondents who were happy amid an extremely difficult time, we attributed it to an indelible optimism and the

TABLE 3.6. Percent Satisfied with Government Response

	Fair/Poor	Excellent/Very Good/Good
Local Officials	22%	75%
State Officials	24%	72%
County Officials	24%	71%
US Congress	43%	63%
President Trump	49%	43%

power of hope. Survivors look forward to the moment of correction, when their lives are back on track and the hard work is behind them. But what happens when the next disaster strikes? Will these communities be prepared to absorb the next punch? Many of our interviewees were not sure that would be the case. Several persons remarked that their neighborhood needed a plan. Something needed to be developed and put into place so the next time disaster strikes, recovery would be different and better.

Considering the many natural disasters this country has faced, why are neighborhoods in Houston, Katy, Port Arthur, Beaumont, Galveston, and beyond asking if their community is prepared for future disasters? How much do we learn and grow each time a city or small town is devastated? We want to explore this critical question in the pages that follow, ultimately asking who is responsible when it comes to community preparedness. How much can local communities shoulder when it comes to preparing for the worst? What does preparedness look like through all phases of a disaster?

4

Anticipation

The clouds darkened and the weather report grew dire. Two days before Hurricane Harvey made landfall in South Texas, every town and city was in a frenzy. Sandbags were filled. Home Depot stores ran out of stock. Citizens lined up at gas stations. The grocery store shelves were sparse, and convenience stores struggled to stock snacks and easy-to-make items. Something was coming. Plans were being made, preparations were taking place, property was being secured, and decisions about what to do next could not wait much longer.

On the other hand, some complacent residents were pretty sure nothing would impact them directly. These "born and bred" Texas Gulf Coast residents assumed Harvey would be just another storm to hit the coastal towns, throwing up some wind and water before blowing past in a couple of days. So many non-events, false alarms, and missed predictions over the years can change a resident's outlook toward disaster warnings. Some residents went through the motions of readiness steps, but in the backs of their minds they assumed Harvey would miss its mark. No one could possibly have been prepared for that much water. No one was ready for that level of destructive flooding. No one had expected the misery that would follow after the water receded, leaving behind water-soaked, mildewed garbage in neighborhoods throughout Houston and Harris County as well as apartment complexes, homes, and mobile home parks in the rural areas of South Texas.

Beth, a British transplant living in West Houston, was one of those complacent residents. Her husband was in the oil business, and they had lived on the coast for the last twenty-five years. In Texas, Louisiana, and Mississippi, they had faced their share of hurricanes and tropical storms, so Harvey was not their first—and in their minds, not their last—brush with disaster. In fact, they tried to put a positive spin on what was expected to be an unpleasant few days. On that Friday evening, Beth invited the family next door over for what she coined a "Hello Harvey" party. Beth prepared a large meal, and as they sat at the dining room table, passed around dishes, and scooped food onto their plates, the couples swapped plans in case either one of their houses flooded. They were enjoying each other's company when a clap of thunder startled them and the rain began to fall. Beth got up from the table to video the storm with her phone. Then she turned back to her dinner guests, shrugged her shoulders, and quipped, "Just a standard rainy evening."

Focusing on the "Hello Harvey" party in Beth's suburban home would offer an incomplete understanding of her disaster experience, though. She and her dinner guests may have laughed on the eve of Harvey, but by the end of the week, her voice had changed. She would say goodbye to neighbors who evacuated. In addition, like so many others, she would turn to the government for recovery assistance. For the first time, she truly understood her family was facing a long recovery period.

However, if we zoom out and try to look at Hurricane Harvey as a monolithic experience, we fail to miss the important details of this disaster story. In a year that produced three back-to-back hurricanes, it is easy to praise the Texas Gulf Coast as resilient and their response and recovery as a success in comparison to the reports coming out of Puerto Rico following Hurricane Maria. If we look at some social indicators of resilience that are established well before disasters strike—such as a sense of community and civic participation—the Texas Gulf Coast appeared to be comprised of strong, vibrant communities capable of withstanding the stress of a natural disaster.

Nevertheless, when we unpacked the data we collected from our interviews, we noticed cracks in this resilience and survivor stories that emphasized this point. Some cracks we found along the social and psychological components of place and race. Trust was not shared equally across African American residents and white residents. Moreover, Latinx residents did not see their towns and cities in the same way that white residents did. Linda, the woman whose son's bike was left behind in the hurricane, shared how the days leading up to Harvey illustrated this racial and ethnic divide. As a Latina who primarily spoke Spanish, Linda felt isolated from her neighbors and struggled to interpret hurricane warnings. We continue to share her story later in this chapter. In other cases, cracks emerged at the intersection of the physical location of communities and their psychological perceptions of hurricane risk. Emma and Claire, who we have yet to introduce, talked about how housing developments and insurance policies amplified hurricane risk and cultivated complacency when it came to hurricane preparedness. To tell the complete story of Hurricane Harvey, we must travel back in time before the hurricane made landfall.

In this chapter, we focus on the pre-event phase of the disaster, which is often marked by assessing the risk of experiencing a hurricane and preparing to evacuate or shelter in place. The pre-event phase (or the time in between recovery and the next disaster) is also about how the social life of a community—our everyday experiences—plays a role in how we respond to disasters and build resilience. To begin, we identify the indicators that suggested the Texas Gulf Coast was both a great place to live and a place that could withstand a hurricane. We then consider how issues of trust, resources, disaster communication, and faulty risk perceptions chipped away at these communities' resilience.

The Community DNA of the Texas Gulf Coast

Like our actual DNA, the composition of communities says a lot about who we are and how we respond to the inevitable challenges that will occur throughout our lives. In their approach to building local resilience to disasters, FEMA refers to this concept as community DNA, which consists of how people interact in their communities, what organizations exist to meet the complicated needs of communities, and what established practices are in place to solve collective problems that communities face during the evolution of natural disasters.[1]

Just as humans have a unique genetic makeup, every community's DNA is different. For example, a suburban community may have several parks and public spaces where residents socialize with one another, but that same community may not have a walkable infrastructure that allows residents to get around without some form of transportation. In contrast, an urban neighborhood may not have an expansive park system, but residents may still feel connected to the community because a local YMCA or community center hosts events and meetings that regularly bring people together. Given the differences across communities, FEMA has endorsed a Whole Community strategy, which argues that a one-size-fits-all approach is neither productive nor effective in fostering community resilience. Instead, FEMA encourages communities to tailor their disaster management plans—from preparedness to recovery—based on their own social-genetic makeup.

Genes predispose certain people to a host of health problems, whereas others appear to be immune or protected from the negative exposure to pathogens or disease. From a community DNA perspective, communities can possess characteristics that may shield them from potential problems like disasters, in effect keeping communities healthy and thriving. On the other hand, some communities may be wired in such a way that they are more susceptible to the negative consequences of disasters. Across the resilience literature, these characteristics—or strands of community DNA—are referred to as adaptive capacities or domains.[2] These capacities include social capital, communication, economic development, and community competence.[3] In this chapter, we will pay particular attention to social capital, communication, and economic development.

Putnam defines social capital as the "features of social life—networks, norms, and trust—that enable participants to act together more effectively to pursue shared objectives."[4] There are three types of social capital: bonding, bridging, and linking social capital. We will explore each of these forms of capital beginning in this chapter and carrying on into chapters five and six. To begin, bonding social capital includes feelings of belonging and identification with a certain group or type of people. Research has shown that individuals who report stronger feelings of belonging in their communities and have lived in their communities longer are more likely to take significant steps toward preparedness.[5]

Overall, the people we talked with revealed that the communities along the Texas Gulf Coast had relatively strong bonding social capital. Over half of all residents living in Houston, Galveston, or elsewhere in Texas (e.g., Beaumont or Port Arthur) either agreed or strongly agreed that people feel like they belong to their community, that people help one another, and that people are treated fairly regardless of their background. The only exception was found in Corpus Christi, where slightly over a third of respondents felt like people belonged and less than half felt that people helped one another and were treated fairly.

As we examined this data more closely, we found that age and income were directly tied to these feelings of connectedness and caring.

For instance, those with higher incomes reported having feelings of a stronger connection to their community than those with lower incomes. Older individuals also felt stronger bonds to the community than younger residents, which may be due to residential tenure or the notion that older individuals have lived in their communities longer. Nevertheless, race, education, and gender were seemingly unrelated to these aspects of bonding social capital.

This strong sense of community was illuminated in the stories people shared with us. Beth certainly felt a connection to her community and, in particular, to her neighborhood. She described her neighborhood as encompassing the human lifespan from infants to nonagenarians. Although she isn't a Houston native, the residential tenure in her neighborhood was relatively robust with what she described as "original owners" and families who had lived there for decades, to the point that multiple generations of families were living around the corner from one another. As she put it, "This means that there is a strong sense of community, with younger families looking out for the senior residents." The neighborhood was also quite social, with backyard movie nights, potlucks, and get-togethers at the local swim club. Her words painted an idyllic scene of a community. She said, "Children played across unfenced front yards and glasses of wine were enjoyed by neighbors." For Beth, the neighborhood was a safe place where families could simply escape from the stressors associated with work and enjoy the company of one another.

We traveled outside of Beth's neighborhood and heard similar sentiments. The people we spoke with wanted to know their neighbors and found informal and formal ways to integrate themselves into the community. In fact, two-thirds of the people we interviewed indicated they spoke several times a week to just about every day with one of their immediate neighbors, and almost half of them had worked with their neighbor in the past year to fix or improve something. These informal ways that residents bonded with one another may not be centered on disasters, but outdoor movie nights and potluck suppers lay an important foundation to help one another in difficult times. Sure, on the surface, a glass of merlot pairs better with a steak on the grill than a discussion about what supplies to include in a home disaster kit, but we suspect that in between sips of wine and the sound of children pedaling their bikes down the cul-de-sac, neighbors recognized that they loved their community and that they would want to help their neighbors if something terrible were to occur.

These informal interactions are also important because the everyday citizen plays an influential role in how residents interpret and respond to potential risks. We may turn to scientists, researchers, and government leaders to inform us about issues like climate change and natural disasters. However, the next-door neighbor who invites us over to their place for a Saturday night BBQ also shapes our understanding of risk when they start talking about this year's upcoming hurricane season and the decision to finally purchase flood insurance. Kasperson and colleagues refer to this phenomenon as the social amplification of risk, which posits that both expert and non-expert sources are influential in how we understand our susceptibility to potential threats.[6] We, the everyday resident, represent a unique strand in our community DNA that may persuade our neighbors or friends to take hurricane threats seriously.

In fact, our next-door neighbors may be more persuasive in shaping risk perceptions because they can be more responsive to local residents' questions and can personalize information to the needs and unique features of a local community.[7] We tend to trust these informal, non-expert sources because they are one of us. We sit next to them on the bleachers at the Friday night football games. We run into them at the neighborhood grocery store. They are our teachers, pastors, and mail carriers. Our proximity to neighbors helps us recognize that if they perceive a disaster to be a threat, then perhaps the disaster is a threat to *us* as well. Unfortunately, everyday conversations may also attenuate risk perceptions. Comments like Beth's "standard rainy evening" or jocular "Hello Harvey" party do not convey the severity of hurricanes. And as we will discuss later in this chapter, the public's understanding of risk can get thrown off-course. Nevertheless, the evidence of frequent neighborly interaction suggested these communities at least had the capacity to amplify risk perceptions.

Survivors' responses to a wide range of questions illustrated an overall perception of the Texas Gulf Coast as a series of caring and connected communities. However, we were also interested in whether or not individuals felt they personally belonged to their communities. Figure 4.1 represents the responses we received when we asked interviewees to select

Figure 4.1. Inclusion in the Community Self Scale. Credit: Aron, A., E. N. Aron, and D. Smollan. 1992. "Inclusion of Other in the Self Scale and the Structure of Interpersonal Closeness." *Journal of Personality and Social Psychology* 63(4):596–612.

which figure most accurately reflected their level of connectedness to the community. The S circle represents them (i.e., the self) and the C circle represents the community. For example, if someone selected the option farthest to the left, they characterized themselves as not belonging to the community or neighborhood groups and did not consider themselves as someone who could make a difference or impact when it comes to local issues. Thus, the picture at far left of two completely separate circles (Option 1) depicts an individual who feels totally isolated from the life of their community. In contrast, the picture on the far right where one circle is practically transposed onto the other circle (Option 6) symbolizes an individual who feels fully immersed in their community. The person who selected Option 6 characterized themselves as being active in local organizations and possessing the level of community involvement and confidence to understand what was happening in their community. Among our respondents, nearly two-thirds selected Options 3 through 6—further evidence that individuals perceived themselves as moderately to fully integrated members of their communities.

In addition to feelings of community belonging, the Texas Gulf Coast appeared to have high levels of civic participation, which is considered a vital community relationship associated with community resilience.[8] Through our interviews, we found that slightly over a third of individuals said they belonged to a charitable organization that provided services to those in need (35.3 percent); followed by volunteering for a youth organization such as Boy/Girl Scouts or a sports league (24.6 percent); a neighborhood association, crime watch group, or trade/business association (23.3 percent); a parent/teacher association or school group (22.3 percent); a hobby, investment, or garden club (21.8 percent); an adult sports league (21.4 percent); and a support group or self-help program for people or their families with specific illnesses, disabilities, problems, or addictions (18.1 percent).

Nearly half of the people we spoke with were members of a church, synagogue, or other religious community. While attendance varied, over half attended religious services at least once or twice a month and 40 percent were actively involved in their religious communities outside of worship services. In total, less than a third of the people we spoke with did not belong to any type of community organization, and half of the survivors we talked with were involved in at least two different types of community organizations. On average, Texas Gulf Coast residents belonged to roughly three community organizations. This level of organizational membership helped establish social networks that residents and organizations could seek out, as well as offer resources to in the case of an emergency. Our findings seemed to support this notion. Specifically, the more organizations residents belonged to, the more likely they were to have a cohort of friends who, in both the four months leading up to Hurricane Harvey and the two months following, had given them material or monetary support (e.g., food, clothes, temporary housing), offered advice, acted as a sounding board, provided transportation, or taken care of them when they were sick.

Despite promising indicators of strong communities, other findings revealed cracks in Texas Gulf Coast resilience. In some instances, these cracks surfaced along racial lines. In other cases, threats to resilience were found among all residents but may have been felt more profoundly across communities of color. After interviewing residents as part of our survey, exploring the Kaiser Family Foundation data,[9] and hearing the stories and narratives told by survivors, the three main resilience cracks to emerge were a lack of trust among black and Latinx residents, communication failures, and a low hurricane risk perception that exposed residents to more dangerous disaster consequences.

Cracks in Resilience: Trust

Perhaps one of the most glaring findings in the data from our interviews was the trust gap among white, African American, and Latinx residents. Through our in-person interviews and online surveys, we found that trust was not equally shared across different racial groups. Specifically, significant differences existed between race and trust when it came to neighbors and people living at their current locations following Hurricane Harvey. Whereas a majority of white residents said they could trust their neighbors (58 percent) and those living at their current locations (e.g., neighborhood, shelters, friends' or relatives' homes, or hotels; 53.6 percent), a majority of African Americans claimed that neighbors (61.7 percent) and those living at their current locations (63.2 percent) could not be trusted.

The trust gap between African American and white residents may be due in part to differences in bridging social capital, which involves social ties that help community members connect across different demographic characteristics like class and race.[10] While civic involvement in community organizations was relatively strong along the Texas Gulf Coast, the racial diversity within the groups was not. We asked those who belonged to a community organization how many people within their group were a race different from them. A significant difference emerged between white and African American residents in their responses. Nearly two-thirds of African American residents (65.7 percent) reported that all or most of the people who participated in the same organizations as them were also black, whereas only half of white residents (51.4 percent) reported they belonged to racially homogeneous groups.

Of course, we weren't able to go into every community organization to confirm the racial heterogeneity of the groups. It may be possible that white residents overemphasized the diversity of the organizations they belonged to because they perceived this response to be more socially desirable. Nevertheless, this finding provides a possible explanation as to why black residents were less likely to trust other people within their communities. Even if white residents overstated the racial diversity of their community organizations, black residents reported they had fewer connections to individuals across different racial groups, which is one indicator of lower bridging social capital. Additionally, we acknowledge the potentially important role that the long-standing historical divide between the white majority and nonwhite minorities might be playing in the interpretation of these findings. Whether through the social forces of homophily or the lingering racial mistrust resulting from a history of civil rights struggles, social connections continue to develop mostly along racial boundaries.

Differences in trust and community perceptions also existed between the Latinx and non-Latinx communities. Latinx residents significantly differed from non-Latinx residents in terms of their perceptions of their community's resilience. Specifically, Latinx residents found their communities to be less caring and possessed fewer resources to help its residents in their daily lives when compared to non-Latinx residents. In addition, Latinx residents were less optimistic about their community's abilities, such as to learn from past setbacks, manage disasters, and share information with the public.

We suspect the political climate in 2017 helped shape the differing perceptions of place between Latinx and non-Latinx residents. Hurricane Harvey was unique in the sense that the storm made landfall in counties where Hispanic residents made up roughly 20–45 percent of the counties' respective populations. Specifically, Harvey hit Houston, the third largest US city with undocumented immigrants[11] at a time when immigration was perhaps the most divisive, front-and-center issue in the American political discourse. Having taken office just eight months earlier, President Donald Trump had spent his presidential campaign and the early months of his administration arguing vociferously for a border wall along the US–Mexico border, railing against sanctuary cities, and wavering on the future status of Deferred Action for Childhood Arrivals (DACA) recipients (children who illegally entered the country with their parents). These national conversations about immigration and American cultural identity transcended the boundaries of the nation as a place and affected how Latinx residents saw themselves within the context of their local communities along the Texas Gulf Coast.

The negative attention, cultural stereotypes, and vitriol being hurled at Central American immigrants in the form of "Build the Wall" chants may have led many immigrants in Linda's neighborhood to keep their heads down and not draw attention to themselves. An immigrant in her thirties, Linda did not describe her community in the same glowing terms others had before her. Whereas Beth fondly described her neighborhood as a place where children played across unfenced yards and neighbors engaged in fellowship, Linda described her town as a "quiet, lonely place lacking in vigilance." She added, "In the town where I lived, the majority were immigrants. It is incredible that one barely knows his neighbor. Most of the time people are busy working and people do not interact with each other." Linda's description of a lonely apartment complex meant her pre-hurricane plans were drastically different from Beth's. Instead of a "Hello Harvey" party where she coordinated evacuation plans with her neighbors, Linda was left without a trusted group of people at a time when many immigrants needed help from a support network.

With President Trump facing his first major natural disaster as president—a disaster that would undoubtedly impact millions of residents, including many undocumented immigrants—rumors circulated about what would happen if immigrants living in the shadows sought help during and after the hurricane. In fact, nearly 40 percent (38.8 percent) of participants who were born in a country other than the US indicated in the Kaiser Family Foundation survey that they were either very worried or somewhat worried that seeking help following Harvey would draw unwanted attention to their or a family member's immigration status. In a 2017 survey of over three hundred undocumented day laborers through the University of Illinois–Chicago Great Cities Institute, nearly two-thirds of the Houston-area participants indicated they were fearful to seek help from the government.[12] Even in our interviews, we asked residents whether they could trust the people (such as government officials) who provided services to hurricane victims. While our results did not yield significant differences, a majority of non-Latinx residents (53 percent) said people who provided disaster services could be trusted, while a majority of Latinx residents (57.3 percent) said they could not be too careful when working with people providing aid. Taken together, the Kaiser Family Foundation, the Great Cities data, and our interviews reveal feelings of isolation from local communities and a lack of trust toward the emergency management officials responsible for ensuring the safety of their communities' residents. As an adaptive capacity of community resilience, social capital is grounded in trust and reciprocity, but the politics of 2017 constructed a place where residents were uncertain of how they would be treated during the disaster.

Linda's story illustrates the social isolation and fear Latinx residents felt as they made crucial decisions about how to survive Hurricane Harvey. As the rain poured down and the winds howled on that Friday night, Linda watched and worried from her first-floor apartment in her predominately immigrant neighborhood. Like Beth, Linda had at first thought it was just going to be a "normal rainy day." However, by early Sunday morning, water was seeping into Linda's apartment. She was desperate. Even though she lived in a place where she was not fully integrated into the life of her community, she knew she could no longer cope with the flooding by herself. She mustered up the courage to climb the stairs of her apartment complex and introduce herself to the two families that lived above her. Linda and her family had lived in their apartment for a year, but this encounter in the initial days of Hurricane Harvey was the first time she had spoken with her upstairs neighbors. While the company of other tenants provided some solace that evening, Linda expressed regret that it took a disaster to finally meet her neighbors. She added, "I think we could have helped each other more on previous days."

After spending part of Sunday night with other families in a second-floor apartment, Linda knew she needed to evacuate. She returned to her residence and frantically waded through dirty water to grab essential documents and a few clothes before a group of volunteers rescued her by boat. During this journey, Linda again heard many of the rumors that circulated in the days before Harvey. Linda recalled, "Some immigrants in a boat wanted to go to the shelter, but they weren't sure where they should go. They were afraid to register to get shelter and food." Linda's story illustrates that distrust can create a place where people don't know who to believe—which, in a disaster scenario, could result in negative consequences. Linda's story also emphasizes the second crack in resilience: communication.

Cracks in Resilience: Communication

Like social capital, communication is an adaptive capacity of community resilience[13] that is central to helping communities cope before, during, and after disasters.[14] Disaster communication can come in the form of formal messages from official sources of information, such as emergency managers and public health officials,[15] or through everyday conversations with fellow citizens who are interested in looking out for their neighbors.[16] Disaster communication is also purposeful in the sense that the messages created and shared with and around the public are intended to achieve certain goals. Before disasters strike, disaster communication is focused on educating and persuading people so they can understand the risks they face and the steps they can take to prepare for what's ahead. During a disaster, communication may still include messages about preparedness, but efforts may also emphasize correcting misinformation and connecting people to appropriate resources and support. To meet these goals, emergency management, public health officials, and disaster service providers must establish relationships with local residents and offer messages across a variety of communication channels. Unfortunately, we found that these groups across the Texas Gulf Coast had not effectively developed robust relationships with the public in advance of Hurricane Harvey and that the information that was shared failed to reach linguistically isolated populations. Another crack in resilience emerged.

Whereas the previous crack in resilience—which pertained to social trust—cut across race, we found that communities struggled to educate and inform all residents, regardless of who they were or where they lived, although some of these failures appear to have been profound when it came to linguistically isolated groups. Nearly half of all the people we interviewed neither believed their community to be the type of place that tries to prevent disasters nor perceived their community to be actively preparing for future disasters. These perceptions may reflect a lack of preparedness on the part of local emergency management; however, the findings also illustrate that municipalities may have preparedness plans in place but have not done an effective job of communicating those preparedness and mitigation efforts to Texas residents. Our data indicated that slightly over a third of residents did not believe their communities provided them with information about what to do in case of a disaster. Given these perceptions, residents sought information from fellow residents. Many turned to family, friends, and neighbors. They checked Facebook pages and watched the local news. But turning to other lay people online for advice was not necessarily the panacea to the information vacuum. Rumors often emerge before, during, and after a disaster, as individuals actively seek information about how to respond. This was certainly the case with Hurricane Harvey. One survivor summarized their experience this way: "No one knew . . . what to believe or not believe." These sentiments were echoed in the stories people told us.

Claire, a new mother of two who never thought in "a million years" that her house would flood, told us, "I think the community didn't do so well preparing its people for the storm, but it did very well responding to the aftermath." Others added, "It could have been much better. No one was prepared at all. No one knew what to do, where to go." Claire had bonding social capital and place attachment. She had grown up in her community and was now raising a family there. As she put it, "It's a small town, but it's home to us." While bonding social capital is important to fostering resilience, it is not enough. It appears that Claire lacked linking social capital, which consists of relationships formed across individuals or groups of different power statuses.[17] In this case, people like Beth and Claire have bonding social capital because they had developed trust among their equals—peers such as neighbors and fellow residents who belong to the same community organizations as them. However, Claire had not established relationships with the local government and emergency management who could have provided her with information on how to assess and prepare for an impending hurricane.

Neither had Alice. Remember Alice, the woman we met the first night we arrived? When we first spoke to her, she said her house was in the midst of repairs due in large part to the release of water from the Addicks and Barker Reservoirs. Residents were not given an advanced warning about the water release, and we suspected that this lack of notice was due in part to an unprecedented amount of rain and a necessary quick decision that the emergency management officials faced. On February 21, 2018, the *Houston Chronicle* reported that by Friday, August 25, the US Army Corps of Engineers projected that both reservoirs would spill into surrounding neighborhoods; yet, despite this forecast, no one shared this information with Alice and other Houstonians.[18] Had Alice known that her street would be transformed into a swamp, she and her husband might not have waited five days to evacuate.

There is no doubt that disaster communication could be improved—in wealthy, predominately white suburbs, in primarily Spanish-speaking communities, and everywhere else in between. Nevertheless, a theme we found across our data was that the communication challenges were particularly frustrating and consequential for non-English speakers. From our own interviews, Latinx residents were significantly less likely to think their communities effectively (a) shared clear and complete information with the public, and (b) managed disasters when compared to non-Latinx residents. These perceptions were supported in a 2019 report from the Houston Immigration and Legal Services Collaborative (HILSC), which identified several communication problems immigrant communities faced across all phases of Hurricane Harvey. While Houston had disaster preparedness guides written in different languages, including Spanish, the materials did not account for lower literacy levels and were difficult to read. Further, the report outlined the need to disseminate preparedness information in a timely manner to non-English media outlets.[19]

These communication challenges were apparent in Linda's disaster story. Unlike most of the Texas residents who responded to our request for follow-up interviews, Linda spoke English as a second language. She turned to the news leading up to Hurricane Harvey, but she struggled to make sense of what to do because most of the news was in English. She flipped to Spanish language stations but felt the hurricane information was lacking. At that point, she grew frustrated. She even expressed to us that Hispanic news was not enough and that the stations were more focused on telenovelas than the real-life drama unfolding outside her apartment. With the rain pouring down, the winds howling, and the water rising in her parking lot, Linda had to find a way to manage her language barrier. So she focused on the pictures from the radar on the weather reports. She watched the Doppler and saw the bright red rotating circles in a time-lapse, which provided the storm's trajectory. Her strategy was imperfect, but she felt it was the best she could do. Months later she told us, "At that time, it would have helped to have more information on prevention and advice on a possible catastrophe, but it was really scarce. When they emphasized it, it was already very late." Linda's struggle to receive clear and understandable information was certainly a problem. To her credit, she knew she was at risk and wanted to learn how to prepare. Others selected a place to live without knowing the disaster risks they faced. In turn, the third crack in resilience emerged.

Cracks in Resilience: Risk Perception

So far, the cracks in resilience we have explored have largely fallen along the psychological dimensions of place. Communities of color did not share the same levels of trust that their white neighbors possessed.

Linking social capital that connected the government to the people was not robust, particularly for the Latinx and immigrant communities. But the final major crack we found in the Texas Gulf Coast rested at the intersection of psychological and geographic components of place. We gathered that residents did not fully understand the severity of Hurricane Harvey not only because of their lack of prior disaster exposure, but also because sprawling development in areas susceptible to floods gave the impression that Texas Gulf Coast residents would be protected from severe disaster consequences.

Researchers hypothesize that one reason why people are underprepared is because they have not experienced the negative consequences of disasters. Or to put it another way, having experienced a disaster—also known as prior disaster exposure—is often cited as a primary motivating factor for individuals to take steps toward preparedness.[20] Public efforts to encourage preparedness have often worked best when referencing disasters that could actually impact residents. Time and time again, we see news coverage of other natural disasters taking place, but we view these events in the abstract. As one survivor from Port Arthur put it in the lead-up to Harvey making landfall, "I remember thinking Hurricane Katrina all over again. I could not believe that in a matter of hours, my community, my family, myself would actually be one of 'those people.'"

A majority of the people we spoke with said they had never experienced the negative consequences of disasters. So it's unsurprising that many residents struggled to see themselves as "those people"—the ones we see on the news, sitting on cots in a shelter or evacuating homes that have become inundated with water. Specifically, over three-fourths of our interviewees had never felt their life was threatened by a disaster, while approximately two-thirds didn't even know of someone in their community that had been killed or injured due to a disaster. For a majority of respondents, their experiences—or lack thereof—led them to believe that Harvey would be an inconvenience but not a devastation. In their view, it certainly would not be fatal.

In regard to disaster experience and households, over half of the people we talked with said they had never experienced property damage due to a disaster, whereas nearly two-thirds had never lost something of sentimental value as a result of a disaster. In fact, less than 10 percent of the people we talked with had ever experienced any of these disaster consequences twice. This may partially explain why Beth described the Sunday after Hurricane Harvey as a surreal day. Even after twenty-five years of living on the Gulf Coast, she had not experienced a hurricane of that magnitude.

Beyond never experiencing the ramifications of a disaster, people along the Texas Gulf Coast may have also felt a sense of immunity buoyed by their interpretation of what it meant to live or not live in a floodplain. At this point, the geographic, political, and psychological dimensions of place intersect. We will address the geographic and political elements of place through an explanation of coastal development and its role in increasing risk and reducing resilience. Legislatively, federal programs like the National Flood Insurance Program and the 2000 Disaster Mitigation Act have encouraged risky coastal development in flood-prone areas while disincentivizing state and local efforts to take responsibility for floods and hurricanes.

For over fifty years, the National Flood Insurance Program (NFIP) has mandated that residents who take out a federal loan to purchase property in a Special Flood Hazard Area must also purchase federally backed flood insurance.[21] Special Flood Hazard Areas are normally determined to be within a hundred–year floodplain, which means the area has at least a 1 percent chance of flooding each year. Despite good intentions, the NFIP and the 2000 Disaster Mitigation Act have several weaknesses, including, but not limited to, their faulty projection of high-risk flood areas and their near-toothless ability to stop risky coastal development.[22]

First, the National Research Council has questioned the accuracy of the hundred-year floodplain for determining actual risk and losses from floods.[23] In fact, an analysis of parts of Harris County where Houston is located revealed that a majority of claims and insured losses spanning a decade of floods were not within FEMA's designated Special Flood Hazard Areas.[24] Second, even after multiple claims are made on properties impacted by floods, the federal government does not have the authority to condemn buildings, require their removal, or deny reinsuring them in the NFIP, although this was partially remedied through the Disaster Mitigation Act.[25] Instead, those decisions mostly fall on the shoulders of state and local authorities, who do not have much financial incentive to take action when developers are willing to come in, purchase the property at low rates, and rebuild. Moreover, state and local authorities rarely foot the bill for the risky development happening in their backyards. While the Disaster Mitigation Act requires state and local governments to pay for a quarter of the relief costs following disasters, the federal government often incurs most of the expenses.

Taken together, the NFIP and the Disaster Mitigation Act have been unable to stop communities from building and expanding in flood-prone areas, which ultimately creates unsafe places. Burby refers to this as the safe development and local government paradox.[26] In trying to make an area prone to disasters safer, the federal government has implemented policies that give potential homeowners the impression that the land is safe to build on when, in fact, this development has actually increased the level of flood risk these households may face. Further, while local governments directly witness their own citizens suffering in a disaster, these same local governments do little to mitigate disasters and instead opt to champion the development that places their residents at risk.

Houston is a prime example of a city that has failed to see the risk they are creating through their development and expansion. Houston's population has grown exponentially in the last three decades, and the city has shirked proposals for new building codes and flood-control projects. Voters have contributed to creating this unsafe place by deciding three times at the ballot box to reject zoning codes.[27] Perhaps voters derive a sense of comfort from the NFIP and see no need to take local measures to mitigate damages.

Here we suspect the psychological dimensions of place intersect with the politics of disaster mitigation programs and the physical location of communities. The NFIP's floodplain delineation wields a psychological double-edged sword for all residents living in coastal communities. For those who have purchased flood insurance due to living in a floodplain, they have placed themselves at greater risk by living in an area susceptible to flooding. Conversely, those who do not live in a FEMA Special Flood Hazard Area may be less inclined to purchase insurance or prepare for disasters because they perceive themselves to not be at risk. We were curious whether individuals who were not mandated to purchase the insurance would spend the money to cover their losses in case a disaster struck. In a previous national survey from FEMA, 21 percent of

US households had purchased flood insurance, and data collected after Hurricane Harvey from the Kaiser Family Foundation illustrated that Texas followed a similar pattern, with 23 percent of households reporting that they had flood insurance. This finding is particularly troubling given the hundred-year floodplain may not be the most valid indicator of flood risk, which was once again confirmed following Harvey.[28] That is, a considerable amount of Harvey's impact happened outside of the floodplain, where individuals were not required or really expected to purchase flood insurance.

Claire and Emma were two of those people who lived outside the floodplain. It had been a busy summer of new beginnings for both of them. Claire had recently given birth to her second child and moved her young and growing family into a new home. From late-night feedings to unpacking boxes to getting some sleep in between all the chaos, Claire didn't feel like she had to add purchasing flood insurance to the list. After all, her family lived outside of the floodplain, and she questioned the likelihood of experiencing a flood. As Claire put it, "Our new home was twenty-five feet above sea level and we did not live in a flood zone . . . We didn't think in a million years that this flood would come through."

Emma was a college student whose family had just wrapped up a year's worth of renovations on a "fixer-upper" about twenty miles outside of Houston. Emma's family had fallen in love with the house and the area even though they had heard the house had flooded a year earlier. Emma and her family did not take the house's history with flooding as an ominous sign of what was to come. Rather, they were puzzled. Emma said, "It was surprising because the neighborhood is not actually in a flood zone." She tried to rationalize the flooding by chalking it up to the fact that "Houston gets a lot of water."

From both Claire's and Emma's initial comments, we noted that the "flood zone" label simplified their understanding of risk. To them, the flood zone designation acted as a line that demarcated danger. On one side of the line was a flood zone that meant residents were more likely to experience floods. On the other side of the line, residents were impervious to them. Unfortunately, that line is blurry. As past research has shown, the hundred-year floodplain is not the most accurate at determining impact, and relying on flood zones is a faulty way to determine risk. Sadly, Claire and Emma were forced to reassess their understanding of risk after their experience with Hurricane Harvey.

Despite neither one of them living in a FEMA Special Flood Hazard Area, too much rain fell. Claire described the water as "inching" up their driveway. Amid this slow-motion nightmare, all Claire and her husband thought they could do was hug one another and pray. Holding onto her husband, she thought, "Everything we invested in and worked so hard for is slowly being taken away from us." Claire's prayers were answered in the sense that the rain stopped and her husband sprang into action to block and soak up the water that had entered their home. But Harvey left an indelible mark on her young family's life—one she still felt when we spoke with her.

Unlike Claire, Emma was not with her family when Harvey made landfall. Instead, she was about five hours away at a conference in Dallas with fellow college students. She knew her family was in Harvey's path, but she reassured herself in the false comfort of not living in a FEMA floodplain. She thought, "Why would water come into our house? I know it flooded before, but they weren't in a flood zone. It would be fine, right?" Emma wanted to confirm her family was okay, so she called her parents, but no one answered. After multiple attempts to make contact, Emma's sister finally picked up only to say, "We're flooding," and hung up. Of course the family was in a frantic race to raise furniture and move belongings to the second floor of their home, but Emma at the time didn't know what to think. Emma's mom estimated that their house took on about a foot and a half of water, which "went through the house like it was a river." For Claire and Emma, it had been a summer of beginnings, but between the unsafe places they lived, the political decisions to allow development there, and the psychological solace they drew from the flood zone label, they knew they would be starting all over again that fall.

From Party to Parting Ways

After a fun night with their neighbors at the unofficial "Hello Harvey" party, Beth and her husband awoke on Saturday morning to a relatively dry neighborhood. The street was damp, and some tree limbs had fallen.

It was nice enough to get outside and take a walk along the Buffalo Bayou. At that point, Beth said, "We were still not really concerned." That all changed on Sunday. Heavy rains from the night before flooded the street behind Beth's house. On that Sunday morning, Beth and her neighbors officially said "Hello Harvey," but instead of partying, they were now parting ways. Beth spent the day hauling belongings to cars in dry parts of the neighborhood and to boats in the areas already under water. Through tears, Beth no longer heard the roar of thunder like she did on Friday night, but instead the roar of airboats. Babies wailed and dogs barked as families made their way out of the subdivision. "It was a surreal day," Beth said. "I lost count of the number of strangers I hugged that day!"

Even after a heart-wrenching day, Beth still considered herself fortunate. She didn't know Linda, Claire, or Emma, but she clearly understood that a long road lay ahead. On the surface, the Texas Gulf Coast had the capacity to foster resilience, with a strong sense of community and membership in community organizations. With the exception of Latinx residents and their perceptions of communities, this capacity was shared across race and place. But a closer examination of what people had to say revealed the cracks in this resilience that created divides in the lead-up to Harvey based on race, ethnicity, and place of residence. There were issues of trust, failures in communication, and faulty risk perceptions.

There are many aspects of any disaster story that are unanticipated. As Hurricane Harvey barreled toward Texas, no one could give a precise estimate of the damage. No one could identify the exact residents who would emerge as hometown heroes. No one could provide the exact date when neighbors would be reunited with one another. Despite the uncertainties that abound during disasters, the cracks in resilience identified in this chapter could all be anticipated and repaired well before Hurricane Harvey. So while disasters may make communities feel a loss of control over their circumstances, there are ways in which communities can take control and build resilience. Later, we offer an agenda to help communities fix these cracks in resilience before the next disaster strikes. Until then, we consider whether these cracks widened to create deep chasms between people and communities as the disaster shifted from the pre-event to event phase. In the next chapter, we follow the boats such as the ones that helped Linda escape or those that escorted Beth's neighbors out of their subdivision to understand how race and place shaped disaster and displacement experiences in the immediate days and weeks following Hurricane Harvey.

5

Who'll Stop the Rain?

The rain pounded against the windshield. The car's wiper blades rhythmically moved back and forth, working desperately to create enough visibility to see a few feet ahead. Ethan gripped the handle on the inside of the car door and nervously looked over at his dad, Larry, as they drove down the interstate heading south back to Houston on Saturday, August 26. Though the father-son duo moved at a snail's pace down the highway, the day before they had cruised through North Texas on the Hotter-than-Hell bike tour. Ethan and Larry had decided to make the trek that weekend despite the forecast because Ethan was heading into his senior year of high school. After all, they might not have another chance to make a memory like this once Ethan moved away to college.

Like Beth, Claire, and Linda, who we heard from earlier, Larry and his wife, Patty, had weathered other storms before—the last one was Hurricane Ike—and they didn't anticipate another out-of-the-ordinary disaster experience. However, as Larry's knuckles turned white from gripping the steering wheel, he wondered if they should have chanced this trip. He also wondered if this hurricane could be a little different from others in his past. This time, after a long trip home, he returned to flooded neighborhoods and neighbors in need of immediate help.

A day earlier, Diane, who we also heard from earlier, left her home in the serene Nottingham Forest subdivision of Houston—an upper-middle-class neighborhood with immaculately manicured lawns and suburban brick homes, some listed at well over a million dollars. She headed in the opposite direction, toward Dallas. The night before, she had received an email from a friend with an ominous prediction: the Houston area would get fifty inches of rain, which would lead to the flooding of a hundred thousand homes. The email ended with a pretty emphatic plea from her friend: evacuate!

Diane took her friend's advice—"even though no one else in Houston appeared to be evacuating at the time," she told us. Unlike Ethan and Larry's odyssey into the eye of the storm, Diane's exodus was mostly uneventful. She pulled out of her subdivision past the brick entryway emblazoned with an *N* and *F* for Nottingham Forest and headed toward an interstate that was not particularly busy. Her evacuation afforded her the opportunity to grab some dinner with her children who had come in from Oklahoma for an extended visit. Over that meal, Diane's children playfully teased her about preparing so thoroughly for the disaster. Diane took the jokes in stride. In her estimate, Hurricane Harvey would not be as awful as the email warning she had received earlier, but she wanted to be on the safe side.

Ethan and Diane—a teenage boy and an empty nester. At first glance, they may not appear to have much in common, yet both were travelers whose paths almost crossed on a stretch of Texas highway that late August weekend. Each of their experiences encapsulates the decisions and challenges Texas Gulf Coast residents faced when confronted with Hurricane Harvey. There is no doubt that Ethan and Diane experienced challenges in the immediate response to Harvey, but their stories are also quite different than others we will reveal in this chapter. For instance, Ethan and Diane do not share Raelynn's narrative of a single mom managing the negative consequences of both a natural and personal financial disaster. And they are also quite different from Will, an African American and recent transplant to the Houston area who—unlike Ethan, Diane, and Raelynn—lacked a social network that could provide robust bonding social capital. And all of their Harvey stories diverged significantly from that of Charles, who deployed to a primarily African American region of the Texas Gulf Coast to assist with relief efforts. Place is where each story diverges.

For Ethan, Diane, and Raelynn, the greater Houston area was a place socially and psychologically constructed of individuals who cared for one another and had deep social ties. In contrast, Will's recent arrival to Houston rendered his view of the Texas Gulf Coast from a physical or geographic perspective. Ethan's and Diane's families were more financially secure in their neighborhoods, while Raelynn and Will were in places of economic constraint. Charles, on the other hand, was not a resident of the place he assisted, yet his story represents how social capital can span geographically. Whether they knew it or not, place played a role in shaping how each of these individuals responded in the days and weeks after Harvey.

The time between their lives before Harvey and their return to a "new normal" represented a metaphoric place, a disaster purgatory of sorts. Time in this disaster purgatory is not equal. One's actual place—be it Houston, Port Arthur, or anywhere in between—helped to determine the pace of recovery. Some made it out of this disaster purgatory sooner than others, due in large part to the amount and types of social capital available to them. Sadly, as we write this chapter, some are still occupying this metaphoric space. Along the road to recovery, survivors met heroes or became heroes themselves. Several maintained their deep faith as churches and other places of worship emerged as important hubs for disaster relief. Others learned that they occupy multiple places at different ecological levels—a nation, a state, a community, and a neighborhood. Across these various levels, some places were more helpful in ushering survivors through their disaster purgatory. To start this part of the story, we first need to review what displacement looked like and the complicated set of challenges people faced depending on the displacement paths they took.

Displaced to Disaster Purgatory

Ethan and Diane survived gusting winds and a relentless downpour of rain, but surviving the physical storm was only the first of many challenges Texas Gulf Coast residents would face immediately following Hurricane Harvey. Earlier, in more detail, we introduced the displaced persons and discussed how certain demographic characteristics were determinants for the various displacement paths people took (e.g., staying in a shelter, staying with a friend or relative, staying in a hotel/motel). Now we describe the challenges people faced due to displacement. A general vexation existed in the majority of the hurricane-ravaged communities. An overwhelming 77 percent of the people we talked with expressed dissatisfaction with their current living arrangement. When we looked more closely at these responses, we found that people were generally dissatisfied with where they were staying. Nearly 80 percent of those who were able to stay in their residences reported dissatisfaction, but approximately three-quarters of individuals who evacuated were dissatisfied as well. Ultimately, it didn't matter whether someone sheltered-in-place or was forced to evacuate to a friend's house, a hotel, or a shelter—they were generally unhappy with their current living arrangements.

While Texas Gulf Coast residents shared a general sense of disappointment with living conditions following Hurricane Harvey, some clear differences emerged in terms of the struggles and inconveniences people faced based on the type of displacement pathway they took. Individuals who were displaced immediately following Hurricane Harvey reported significantly more challenges with their current living arrangement than individuals who were not forced to evacuate. People who stayed with friends or relatives or who were able to find a FEMA-approved hotel reported an average of four problems with where they were staying. Individuals displaced at shelters indicated an average of approximately two problems that noted their dissatisfaction. Finally, residents staying at home reported less than one daily hassle (problem) on average, despite the inconvenience of the storm and all it brought with it.

Regardless of where people stayed, noise was the most common complaint. With noise as the exception, the types of hassles also varied across different displacement scenarios. Individuals who were homeless prior to Harvey, or who did not have a friend or relative to assist them, turned to FEMA-supported, Red Cross–run shelters. Like other types of displacement, noise and lack of privacy were noted problems. However, the most frequent complaint from those staying in these shelters was the behavior of others. Our respondents complained about not only individuals managing the shelters but those staying in them as well. This hassle appeared to be an impetus for getting out of the shelter as soon as possible—either by force or by choice. For instance, Linda—who you'll remember was forced out of her apartment as the water rose all around her—evacuated to a shelter set up by a local church. She was relieved to have a place to stay, but she soon realized her sojourn would be cut short. "We only stayed there for two days because they evicted us and asked us to go back to our homes," she explained. "They had enough food and clothes, but the pastor's wife kicked us all out. We obviously could not return home since the water remained stagnant in our neighborhood for more than fifteen days." In contrast, an evacuee in another shelter felt well-attended to by those managing the facility. However, the shelter was a disaster purgatory itself. Hell was being stranded on the streets of Houston during Hurricane Harvey. Here, at least, he was safe with a roof over his head. But the place sure wasn't heaven. Hot. Loud. People running around. As he put it, "I couldn't wait to get out."

The stories we heard and the complaints leveled by survivors about their shelter experiences were not unlike what we heard from homeless persons who regularly endure the shelter cycle. These places are often crowded and noisy. People act out and get sick. And people who need the shelter often experience a level of intense anxiety as a result. It doesn't matter if the Salvation Army is running the shelter or another nonprofit service provider; the scene is familiar and the complaints are common in shelters across the United States.

The homeless shelter formula is complicated, and the physical limitations often create significant social and health (physical and mental) challenges that deter potential clients. For good reason, some people in America choose to sleep in the woods, abandoned buildings, or their cars. Though the number of emergency shelter beds can be severely limited in certain cities, for many potential clients, the peace and quiet they find at night lying down by themselves, regardless of where it is, trumps the chaos and confusion that often accompanies the shelter experience. Those persons who were homeless before Hurricane Harvey had a significant reluctance to enter into the temporary FEMA shelters that were being constructed. They knew the conditions would be harsh if they stayed on the streets, but they were as concerned about losing their possessions to theft as much as they were concerned about losing those same possessions to the rising waters.

Individuals who turned to family, friends, and neighbors for a place to stay may have avoided the uncertainty that comes with being surrounded by strangers, but it did not guarantee their living arrangements were comfortable. Half of respondents who stayed with someone they knew complained that a lack of privacy was a significant problem. More than a third of those people also felt the space where they stayed was too small, which led to overcrowding. For those individuals who were accustomed to the privacy of their own homes or apartments, sharing space was becoming more than just an adjustment. The constant couch surfing in an effort to look for the perfect arrangement seldom works.

All that happens over an extended period of time is that people begin to erode what little social capital they have. Social resources deteriorate to the point where friends and family are stretched so thin that they can no longer help, and survivors often find themselves in a precarious living circumstance, not unlike what many homeless persons face each and every day.

Even the individuals who felt they could stay in their own residences recognized that the first few days after the storm were not comfortable. Respondents who stayed put told us that with the exception of noise and other miscellaneous problems, the main issue they faced was an infestation of dirt and bugs. In the days following Harvey, the temperatures were rather cool compared to the usual late August temperatures, which could be as high as the mid-90s in the Houston area. People found rooms without water damage and slept on the floors with the windows open to take advantage of the relatively mild temperatures. Showers were a luxury. Instead, people filled bathtubs with water to be used for sponge baths and to fill toilet tanks. One survivor equated her experience in the immediate days following Harvey to that of roughing it in the wilderness. "We made do," she said. "Basically, it felt a lot like camping." Ultimately, residents were uncomfortable with the interruption Hurricane Harvey caused. Whether displaced or not, residents looked for help in all sorts of places to alleviate their pain and to help them escape their disaster purgatory. As the Department of Homeland Security noted following Hurricane Harvey, "Individuals in the community are always the first true responders in disasters."[1] Based on the responses from people we interviewed, residents did turn to their fellow survivors for immediate help.

Hometown Heroes

From the stories people shared and from the Kaiser Family Foundation survey responses, we gathered that Texas Gulf Coast residents provided a Tale of Two Responses. That is, local communities and their residents were hailed as heroes, while the federal government and its employees were often cast as villains—the all-too-often-heard roadblock to recovery.

Interviewees described a collective healing approach to disaster response and recovery, through which residents drew upon several preexisting resources embedded within their social system to help one another cope.[2] By no means does local collective healing relieve state and federal disaster management agencies from their obligation to provide services to disaster survivors. However, collective healing may augment disaster management efforts, fill in the gaps when disaster management agencies become overwhelmed, or make outreach possible with hard-to-reach populations. For instance, communities may have civic or volunteer organizations that can be critical information sources for residents who are struggling to apply for disaster assistance. These organizations may also volunteer or provide their own donations while people wait for monetary assistance from the federal government.

In addition to established community organizations, local residents can be important assets in a post-disaster landscape. As Fullilove and Saul argue, the "greatest resources for recovery are community members."[3] First, local residents have an understanding of the unique needs of their neighborhood that a federal employee deployed to the region might not possess. For example, Beth described earlier that her neighborhood looked out for its elderly neighbors. Second, local residents may have an emotional connection to their community—a sense of belonging—that motivates them to help their fellow neighbor. This was certainly the case for Ethan.

Ethan and Larry arrived home from their bike race just in time for Larry to grab his scrubs and rush off to the local emergency room where he worked. Fortunately, their house had not flooded yet, but as the rain intensified, water crept into their neighborhood along the edges, into people's backyards, and slowly down the main streets. Ethan traded in his bike from the road race for the family's fishing kayak and paddled over to flooded neighbors' homes to see if they needed anything. He would dock his kayak, jump out, and go into his neighbors' houses to help them move their furniture to higher ground. In a more dramatic instance, he assumed the role of a one-man search-and-rescue team after a neighbor alerted him that her little boy had gone outside to play in the water and hadn't returned home. This was not how Ethan imagined the start of his senior year of high school, but that was the ethos of the neighborhood. Ethan's mom, Patty, described her community as "very friendly, filled with people who would help one another." So that's exactly what Ethan did: helped his neighbors.

Ethan's story is just one of many examples of social capital in the immediate wake of Hurricane Harvey. One survivor said, "Immediately following Harvey, so many people were coming together to help those in need. People opened their homes to displaced families and donated whatever they could." In her Nottingham Forest subdivision, Diane's neighbor opened up a "store" in their living room. In order to ease both the financial burden as well as the time it would take to run from grocery stores to home improvement stores, this neighbor solicited food and supplies from fellow residents that people might need in a pinch. Neighbors could go online, look at the neighborhood's "shopping list," and then purchase supplies to donate to the store. In turn, those in need could stop by the house-turned-storefront and take whatever supplies they needed for free. Beth's neighborhood also had these pop-up stores, and the supplies were abundant. "The supplies that were available covered all items from generators to toothpaste, clothes to toaster ovens, and everything in between!" she said. The local moms' club to which Beth belonged also assisted by coordinating a meal train and offering to take care of people's pets while they navigated the immediate circumstances of recovery.

Indeed, Texas Gulf Coast residents were crucial to the disaster response and recovery. They opened their hearts and homes to the residents most impacted by Harvey. They harnessed existing resources in creative ways. Simply put, they were hometown heroes. This is not surprising given that past research has revealed that bonding social capital, which refers to feelings of belonging with friends and family who are similar to one another,[4] is often accessed first in the immediate aftermath of disasters as people turn to those they know and trust.[5] Nevertheless, the narratives people shared with us also illustrated a potential "dark side" to bonding social capital.[6] Bonding social capital is common in proximal and homogenous networks. When these networks are economically homogenous, it may be difficult to facilitate bridging social capital to communities of different socioeconomic statuses. Though well intentioned, the Nottingham Forest "store" was probably only reached the residents of that subdivision or people connected to someone who lived in that subdivision. Therefore, the resources in the Nottingham Forest "stores" were kept within their neighborhood and distributed to people who were certainly financially impacted by the hurricane, but by no means people who were in the direst of economic straits before Hurricane Harvey. By concentrating resources in an advantaged area rather than sharing resources with more vulnerable places, bonding social capital may act as a mechanism for building resilience within a hyperlocal place like a neighborhood or a subdivision—particularly one that is economically secure or politically well connected—at the expense of fostering resilience for the community as a whole.

Ultimately, while bonding social capital plays an important role in disaster response, bridging and linking social capital are also needed to help people move through the response and recovery efforts. While the stories people shared with us confirmed the notion that local residents can be the greatest assets for a community's ability to recover, they were not the only measure of a community's strength. In the next section, we will explore how places of worship also played a critical role in the response and recovery efforts.

Keeping the Faith

Beyond individuals, community organizations like churches and other faith-based organizations sprang into action to assist Hurricane Harvey survivors. Faith-based groups regularly play an active role in disaster recovery. In their manual, *Building Community Resilience for Children and Families*, Gurwitch and colleagues identify faith-based groups as an important piece of the community resilience puzzle, particularly because these groups "are commonly the first source of support for residents seeking help and information after a disaster."[7] Faith-based groups' role as a conduit of information was twofold in the greater Houston area. With listservs and social media that reached members with a click of a button, churches were able to mobilize volunteers and alert congregants in need of information on how and where to get help. One of the people we spoke with utilized her church as a way to help her community following Harvey. "My local church went into action as soon as it was safe to be outside," she said. "We served meals, handed out clothing, and provided essential toiletries to families in need." Another resident who felt like the federal and state government had initially left survivors as "sitting ducks" did not feel that sense of abandonment. She added, "They [the church] let us know as a community we would all be okay."

As previously discussed, churches had a familiar presence in the Texas Gulf Coast. Almost half of the people we spoke with belonged to a church, synagogue, or other religious community. Furthermore, their membership was not in name only. Over 50 percent of the people we interviewed attended their place of worship at least once or twice a month, and nearly just as many described themselves as active members within the churches' different outreach ministries. Several people also emphasized the importance of faith in helping them weather the storm. Reflecting on how her daughter's young family coped, one survivor said, "Faith in God was the only thing that helped them at all." Another survivor mentioned, "Prayer is the only stress reliever." Others turned to their church for financial help; some sought spiritual counseling.

For people of color and immigrant communities, the role of religion following natural disasters is particularly central to their recovery. Individually, nonwhites are more likely than whites to turn to prayer as a coping mechanism following disasters.[8] For immigrants, churches often serve as a bridge that either provides information about their community or connects individuals to other resources that might not otherwise be readily available.[9] Our interviews confirmed the important relationship between nonwhite residents and their places of worship following disasters.

By now, it is clear that disasters present disruptions to people's everyday life. People evacuate or relocate. Some may be unable to return to work. For some hourly workers, income stops flowing into bank accounts. But for nonwhite residents after Harvey, religion—particularly involvement in organized religion—was seen as a constant amid a sea of interruptions. A larger portion of nonwhites either sustained their participation with a faith-based group or found a new religious community to fulfill their spiritual needs after Hurricane Harvey compared to whites.

Specifically, nearly half of nonwhites were attending religious services in the two to three months following Hurricane Harvey, in contrast to less than a third of whites. Likewise, almost half of the nonwhite respondents said they had participated in events such as a church supper or a bible study since Hurricane Harvey, which was considerably higher than it was for white respondents. The relationship between places of worship and people of color is particularly important to consider in disaster recovery given that our data revealed nonwhites were more likely to be displaced to a shelter, reported more property damage, and experienced more delays in formal disaster relief assistance than whites.

The degree of religiosity along the Texas Gulf Coast and particularly the sustained participation among nonwhite residents in the months immediately following Hurricane Harvey presented an opening for Charles and his organization, the Austin Disaster Relief Network (ADRN). This nonprofit organization, which began in 2009, was able to provide assistance with emergency housing, supplies, resources, and other practical relief from the devastation that people were experiencing all along the Texas Gulf Coast. The ADRN is what some experts would refer to as an *ecological hub* and a form of translocal bridging social capital. Acting as a nerve center for community recovery following disasters, an ecological hub is an organization that other individuals and groups can draw upon to connect with others, share ideas, and partner with one another to maximize a community's ability to heal.

Comprised of 185 churches in the greater Austin, Texas, area, the ADRN's mission is to build public-private partnerships among churches, government, and businesses, particularly as they relate to disaster relief. Simultaneously, the ADRN serves as translocal social capital, providing support that is located in a different geographic place than the area exposed to disaster.[10] Translocal social capital serves an important function during disasters because these reservoirs of support are not directly impacted by the disaster and may have the ability to offer resources without needing help themselves. Located two hours away from Houston, the ADRN did not experience a direct hit by Harvey, but it was still close enough to support the affected areas.

Charles and his team faced a critical decision. With a huge swath of Texas impacted by Harvey, where would their organization go first? As national media descended upon Houston, they decided to focus on "cities that won't likely be in the limelight. Cities like Port Arthur, the Golden Triangle area, Rockport, and other smaller communities." Charles recognized that larger cities would get the majority of the country's attention, and he assumed metropolitan Houston would have the FEMA resources to help those in need. Perhaps he read the minds of some of the people we interviewed—the ones who told us that the further one moved away from the Houston center, the slower the disaster response was. Furthermore, he believed that the neighborhood church was a critical linchpin in smaller communities' survival and recovery. As he put it, "We made the decision to support churches in those communities because the church is always going to be in that community, but for us, the real question was going to be, do these churches have the capacity to help those impacted by this type of major natural disaster?"

When we spoke with Charles, it was clear that the ADRN was the spoke in the wheel to disperse positive energy as well as emotional and material support to Texas Gulf Coast churches trying to meet the needs of those who came looking for help. His organization provided churches with gift cards for gas and groceries to distribute at their discretion to hurricane survivors. For larger financial requests, such as to repair homes, purchase cars, or pay rent and utilities, individuals could go to local churches and complete applications that the ADRN would review. When an application was approved, Charles and his team would provide money to the church that submitted the application. As Charles put it, "The church would then become the assistance broker for persons needing help in recovery." Unbeknownst to him, previous research on social capital following disasters supported his strategy to provide resources to small churches, who in turn could help their community's residents. Following disasters, residents of all economic strata may tap into bonding social capital from their friends, family, and neighbors in close proximity to them; however, over time, inequalities emerge in the amount of social capital received, as higher-income residents are able to tap into translocal ties and lower-income residents are limited to the support within their proximal networks.[11] By funding local churches, Charles ensured resources would not be exhausted for an organization that would most likely be tapped by lower-income families.

As an ecological hub, the ADRN served as an excellent example of bridging social capital, connecting individuals and other organizations to resources that may not have been readily available to them within their immediate social circles. Charles understood that partnerships would be key to his organization's success. He described how many churches, mayors, and other service organizations worked with the ADRN. Over two hundred businesses joined the cause, and even truckers helped by driving supplies for free. "The list [of helpers] is so huge," Charles told us.

Despite being an amalgam of local places of worship, businesses, and a regional network deployed to a community that was not theirs, Charles and his team at the ADRN wanted to ensure that the assistance still felt local. Volunteers may have been from Austin, but on September 30, 2017, they were all residents of Port Arthur. At 3:30 that early fall morning, against a clear, black sky, members of the nearly two hundred churches and businesses affiliated with the ADRN gathered in a parking lot to travel down to Port Arthur. Cups of coffee were distributed to the volunteers who boarded the army of charter buses that would drive them to the heart of Harvey's destruction. While the volunteers initially arrived rubbing their tired eyes, they were quickly brimming with purpose.

Charles wanted his volunteers to communicate that "we're here for you, we love you, and we haven't forgotten you." He arranged for the volunteers to wear heather grey shirts with Port Arthur's Memorial High School colors of red and black instead of the organization's usual yellow uniforms. "Love Port Arthur" and "#PAStrong" were prominently displayed across the fronts of the shirts, with an outline of the state of Texas replacing the *o* in *Love*. By the time nearly a thousand volunteers arrived at Memorial High School, the sun had risen and a bright new day was beginning. Over the course of that day, Hurricane Harvey survivors had their physical, spiritual, and emotional needs met.

Across the parking lots that led into the football stadium and gymnasium, volunteers and hurricane survivors—black and white, female and male, young and old—huddled together in prayer, holding hands, heads bowed, and in some cases, genuflecting. Yellow striped tents commonly found at football tailgates shaded the rows of tables filled with neatly folded clothes. Forklifts drove by with pallets of bottled water. In the distance, children laughed as they jumped up and down in bounce castles and flew down inflatable slides. Other children sat at tables and played board games like Chutes and Ladders and Candy Land with the volunteers. For some of these Port Arthur children, this was the first time in weeks that they hadn't thought about the hurricane and were allowed to simply be kids again.

"These people felt forgotten," Charles explained, but on that sunny Saturday in September, Port Arthur residents felt like themselves. They weren't case numbers waiting for their claims to be processed. They weren't burdens to well-intentioned but overworked caseworkers. For this reason, Charles summed up the experience by saying Love Port Arthur was a "special day." Nevertheless, by that evening, the tents that covered a makeshift thrift store had been torn down. The bounce castles and slides had deflated. The caravan of charter buses hauling volunteers was headed back to Austin. Port Arthur residents were temporarily buoyed by the generosity and compassion of the ADRN, but they needed more than one day of emotional and material support.

As we will discuss in more detail in chapter six, Port Arthur is an exemplar of why place and race matter in disaster recovery. The town's population was decimated, and the city did not receive adequate recovery funds. Slightly more than 30 percent of all residents live in poverty. Charles and his team would continue to work with local churches in the coming months, but translocal social capital from out-of-town nonprofit organizations was not enough. People were also looking to the state and federal government. However, as we looked at data from the Kaiser Family Foundation and spoke with people about their experience with the state and federal government, we realized what Charles meant when he said the people felt forgotten.

A Tale of Two Responses

The previous examples of hometown heroes were vivid and easy to recall for the people we interviewed. The ability to personally witness social capital in the hours and days following the disaster may explain why most of the people we talked with and those who responded to the Kaiser Family Foundation survey viewed the local response to Hurricane Harvey more favorably than the response they had seen from the US Congress, the White House, and the State of Texas. Views on Congress and its handling of Hurricane Harvey were split, with nearly half describing legislators' response as favorable and slightly less than half viewing congressional action unfavorably. Similarly, reaction to President Trump's response was divided; more than 40 percent of respondents approved and over half disapproved. In contrast, nearly three-quarters of the people we interviewed indicated a favorable view of their city and town officials' response to Harvey.

Given the current state of political polarization in the US, we wanted to know if political leanings would help explain these mixed reviews for

Congress and President Trump compared to the overwhelmingly positive reviews of the local response. Indeed, political party affiliation appeared to be an important factor in how people viewed the congressional and presidential responses to Hurricane Harvey. Specifically, only about 10 percent of Republicans thought President Trump's handling of the disaster was fair or poor. Conversely, three-quarters of Democrats and over half of all independent and third-party voters held a negative view of the White House's response. Partisanship aside, across Republicans, Democrats, and Independents, Texas Gulf Coast residents expressed significantly higher levels of satisfaction with local disaster response than federal disaster response. This means that even if Republicans were more inclined to support the efforts of President Trump or the Republican-led Congress on a normal day, Republicans still gave higher marks to their city and county officials than state and federal ones post-disaster.

Overall, these results caught our attention because they followed a somewhat similar pattern to Harvey's most comparable preceding hurricane—Hurricane Katrina. A 2005 *Washington Post*/Kaiser Family Foundation survey of Hurricane Katrina evacuees reported that President George W. Bush had the highest disapproval ratings for his response to the hurricane, followed by the Louisiana state government, and finally, the local government of New Orleans. Given the magnitude of Katrina's impact and the failures at multiple levels of government back in 2005, Texas Gulf Coast residents' disapproval of the federal and state government following Hurricane Harvey seems rather tepid in comparison. Even so, the results illustrate that disaster survivors appear more inclined to approve of local efforts over those of federal and state governments. The survey data does not reveal whether this dissatisfaction with federal and state disaster management was due to an unrealistically high expectation of federal and state government capabilities to assist residents during and after a disaster. However, the conversations we had with residents illustrate that, whether fair or unfair, an expectation gap existed between what residents thought FEMA *should* do and what they actually *did*.

Raining Down Red Tape, Flooded with Forms

If the federal government was consistently viewed less favorably in regard to their handling of Hurricane Harvey, then it is unsurprising that FEMA emerged as the chief adversary in many of the stories shared with us about people's experiences in the immediate days and weeks following Hurricane Harvey. From the first day we arrived in Houston, we noted problems with the way things were being run. When we talked with FEMA workers who had been in the shelters for the last month, no one had an appreciation for the chaos they were trying to corral or the relationships they were trying to maintain. At best, the inter-organizational network between FEMA, the local government, nonprofit service providers, and the Red Cross seemed frayed.

As the foil to the hometown heroes we previously described, FEMA fast became the poster child for bureaucratic incompetence—well-intentioned but slow-moving. One survivor put it bluntly: "FEMA was difficult. Defunct. Disorganized." People we spoke with shared their interactions with FEMA, and even those who had not personally been in touch with FEMA still had strong opinions about the agency based on what they had heard from other survivors. Thus, the myth of FEMA as a failure was perpetuated along the Texas Gulf Coast. We would be remiss if we didn't mention that some of the people we spoke with did express gratitude for the help they received from FEMA. Some also recognized that given the devastating hurricane season with Hurricanes Irma and Maria following Harvey, the federal government was stretched and could only do so much in a short period of time.

However, among the people we interviewed, the chief complaints leveled at FEMA seemed to be a perceived lack of federal presence, confusing forms, and long waiting periods. First, people we spoke to indicated that—from at least what they could tell—the federal government's response in their community was nonexistent. However, we must emphasize that this was simply several people's perception. In fact, as of November 2017, in the fifty-three counties designated for individual or public assistance, over thirty-five fixed or mobile disaster recovery centers were established. Additionally, FEMA set up thirty-six donation centers, eleven volunteer reception sites, nine food banks, and fifteen feeding sites. Clearly, FEMA had a presence along the Texas Gulf Coast even if some residents did not perceive the direct impact of their assistance.

Second, FEMA was described as confusing, which may have stemmed from FEMA's operation as an outsider coming to the rescue of a community it did not know. As the federal government has suggested with their efforts to implement Whole Community disaster management approaches, it is not reasonable for even a well-intentioned organization like FEMA to understand the community DNA of every potential town it may eventually assist. Consequently, federal efforts to help local residents may not be as streamlined as residents would like them to be, primarily because it takes time to get FEMA on the ground in the disaster area, establish disaster recovery centers, and address the emerging needs of survivors.

Diane certainly felt this way. Unlike several of the people we spoke with whose words dripped with disdain for the government agency, Diane was rather diplomatic in her assessment of FEMA. She was happy she could request assistance from her smartphone while she sat on the edge of her hotel bed in Dallas. She also described FEMA's website as functional and their presence extensive in the Houston area. Nevertheless, Diane found the FEMA lodging reimbursement process to be "unnerving," partially due to FEMA "not knowing anything about Houston." Diane wanted to make sure she could be reimbursed for evacuating to a hotel, so she had checked to make sure she was at a "FEMA hotel" that would qualify for that type of reimbursement. Space was limited at many of these hotels, and Diane found herself moving from one hotel to the next. Diane spent several hours trying to communicate with FEMA to find out why she and her family had to migrate to different hotels, but each contact with FEMA grew more and more frustrating as a new FEMA representative asked Diane for the same information over and over.

Beth, who told us her story when we first arrived in Houston, had a "distressing" experience with FEMA. Even though Beth described her neighborhood as a place where families looked out for one another, Harvey's wrath required her to seek additional assistance outside of her social network. So Beth turned to FEMA. However, she felt the language on the initial forms was confusing. She took a break from filling out the forms, but when she returned to complete the paperwork online, she had trouble accessing her case on FEMA's website. After several failed attempts to locate her family's information, the company that Beth's husband worked for stepped in and helped them find temporary accommodations. This was just one example of how people felt their personal networks helped them recover faster than the federal government.

Beth was fortunate to have the necessary social capital to get help when the federal government presented her with confusing information or did not move at the pace she needed. Unfortunately, many of the people we spoke with did not have family members to turn to for financial help or friends to stay with while their houses were being repaired. Even if people initially relied on family and friends, it was possible for them to exhaust all of their bonding social capital, which is normally the first type of social capital tapped following a disaster.[12] Those at a relative disadvantage may have had an immediate proximal network that was also at an economic disadvantage and therefore of limited assistance. As Elliott and colleagues note, equal access to social capital begins to deteriorate over the lifespan of a disaster as disadvantaged groups deplete their bonding social capital and lack the ties to connect with other resources in and around where they live.[13]

Turning to FEMA seemed like some people's only option, and amid all the stress that comes with disaster recovery, seeking help from what was perceived as a slow-moving agency was not ideal. This sentiment was evident in the words of Ethan's mom, Patty. After all Patty and her family had been through, she described her thoughts following Harvey not as feelings of elation for surviving a disaster but as a crushing feeling. Patty coined it "flood guilt." Unlike nearly half of the people from the Kaiser Family Foundation survey, Patty and her family had purchased private flood insurance before the storm, and this decision proved to be a wise one. Patty described the insurance process post-Harvey as efficient and felt bad as she heard from other residents about their feelings of frustration after filling out and filing FEMA forms.

Rumors had circulated that the FEMA process required a great deal of time, energy, and patience, with little return on investment. This description sounded so unappealing to some that they were discouraged from seeking help from FEMA in the first place. As one survivor put it, "I could not stomach spending forty-plus hours on this [applying for FEMA aid] and sending in sixty-plus pages to be denied. We've given up on [FEMA] doing anything productive."

Raelynn, who we met earlier, a single mom raising her daughter, had also heard that the lines to receive help at the FEMA disaster recovery center were long, and that the people waiting to get help would have to "endure the weather outside for many hours." Unlike other respondents,

Raelynn couldn't forgo seeking help from the federal government even if the wait was inconvenient. Just a week before Hurricane Harvey became a natural disaster to Texas Gulf Coast residents, Raelynn and her family experienced a financial disaster of their own. Raelynn's boyfriend lost his job, and the family surmised that they would have to be frugal with their spending until he found employment. Then Harvey happened. Their house was destroyed, her car was flooded, and they could no longer wait for a second source of income. The days following Harvey were stressful for Raelynn. As much as she was willing to wait in lines at the recovery centers, she didn't know if it would be possible to wait for hours when she needed to drop off and pick up her daughter from school and look for an additional job to assist with the repairs and cleanup.

Despite her trepidations about navigating the reams of FEMA paperwork on top of her responsibilities as a parent and primary earner, Raelynn was able to get $500 in assistance through FEMA about a month after Hurricane Harvey. Two months after she received that financial assistance, a FEMA representative inspected the damages to Raelynn's house and found an Airbnb for Raelynn, her boyfriend, and her daughter. She admitted the space was rather tight for the three of them, but Raelynn put this inconvenience in perspective. For many Texas Gulf Coast residents, a cramped space was the least of their worries. Thousands had nowhere to go and had no one to ask for help.

In Search of Help

After interviewing Texas Gulf Coast residents three months following Hurricane Harvey, the Kaiser Family Foundation concluded that needs still had not been met. Broadly, the foundation reported that "nearly half of those who suffered losses across the region say they are not getting the help they need to recover."[14] Perhaps more striking, this trend continued across different categories of assistance. Specifically, more than half of those applying for disaster assistance said they needed more help. Nearly three-quarters of people whose vehicles were destroyed needed more help finding transportation. From a health perspective, slightly over half of participants in need of medical care or professional counseling expressed the need for more help. Housing was another category requiring more assistance, as damaged houses remained vacant all over Texas coastal neighborhoods. Two-thirds of residents reported needing more help in finding temporary housing, while approximately three-quarters of those looking to find a new, affordable place to live were struggling for assistance. As we might have predicted, housing assistance varied based on place.

For instance, Diane recounted that the residents of her middle-class Houston subdivision experienced some housing struggles—three houses were up for sale and two were sitting as vacant lots. However, Diane's neighborhood was in the process of recovery and did not reflect the stagnation described earlier. Diane explained that of the thirty homes that flooded, two had already been repaired, while twenty-one homes were in the process of being repaired. We certainly do not want to minimize Diane's neighbors' experiences and the stress that comes with rebuilding and repairing homes in a post-disaster landscape. However, Diane's account of the reconstruction process contrasts with other places along the Texas Gulf Coast. We extrapolate from Diane's account that there is both a strong sense of community and place attachment to her subdivision. People felt connected enough to their property that two-thirds of the residents in damaged homes were motivated to stay and pay for repairs, whereas Linda was confident that she would move because her psychological construction of place was of a "lonely community lacking in vigilance." She lived in an apartment complex, but for her, it was hardly a community. Remember, she met her neighbors for the first time when she and her family evacuated. Diane's subdivision was rebuilding, but Linda was "starting over from scratch in every single way."

Diane's subdivision was also fortunate because they could make the necessary repairs only months after Harvey. Financial hardship was another challenge identified in the Kaiser Family Foundation survey, and the findings helped to illuminate the stories people shared with us. In particular, almost two-thirds of people who said they needed to find a job following Hurricane Harvey expressed the need for more assistance in doing so. A couple of people we spoke with explained that they paid for repairs or hotel stays out of pocket and were waiting for reimbursement from FEMA or their insurance agent.

Consequently, those out-of-pocket costs for many residents depleted their savings accounts. As one survivor put it: "Try having your home devalued to half its price and then have to spend an additional $300,000 on getting it fixed out of pocket. And have your income remain the same. That's stressful. Emotional." One person we spoke with said the financial strain after Harvey forced him to make some really tough decisions. As he explained, "People are still struggling between the choices of food for the family or sheetrock for the home."

This mix of exasperation and despair over seeking financial help following Harvey was perhaps felt most strongly in our conversation with Will, an African American man who described himself as relatively new to the Houston area. As newcomers to southeast Texas, Will and his wife did not have a local support network to turn to and initially evacuated to a Red Cross shelter. When the shelter closed, Will and his wife had nowhere to go, so they slept in their car from November 2017 to February 2018. Will and his wife eventually received some assistance, including a $25 gift card to a local supermarket chain and some support from Fort Worth Catholic Charities, but this support was simply not enough. Will grew frustrated that he couldn't even meet his most basic needs, and we could sense in his response that as much as he needed financial help, he also needed people to understand his pain and sense of hopelessness. At one point he said, "Man, I can't even afford a roll of toilet paper today. Do you know how that feels?" Will's story, among several other narratives, highlighted that for many, the road to recovery was still very long.

The Marathon

The same nervous feeling Ethan had felt during his August 26 tempestuous trip back to a flooded Houston surfaced once more. Despite the real needs that still existed along the Texas Gulf Coast, people tried to get back to a routine. For Ethan, this meant starting his senior year of high school. The return to school brought consistency back to a life interrupted by Harvey. But this school day was different. Ethan was called to the principal's office. He struggled to imagine what this request could be about as he strolled down the hallway lined with lockers. When he walked into the principal's office, he came face-to-face with an envelope and an administrator befuddled as to why a student would receive mail addressed to the school. Ethan tore open the envelope to discover a thank-you card from an elderly couple he had rescued on his fishing kayak that late August weekend. In humble fashion, Ethan stuffed the note in his backpack and didn't bring it up to his parents, but Ethan's mom, Patty, eventually found the note. When she described this as an experience that stuck out to her following Harvey, we could tell she was bursting with pride for her son. At the same time, Patty acknowledged that Ethan's bravery and altruism were admirable but not extraordinary. She added, "He is just one of the many people that helped out during this time of chaos and confusion."

We've been describing in these pages how bonding social capital, perceived connectedness to the community, and networks of individuals and organizations provided material support in the initial days following Hurricane Harvey. However, bonding social capital was not sustainable to help residents in the weeks and months ahead. In fact, we have argued throughout this chapter that bonding social capital may have widened the recovery gap between residents based on the places they lived. For those in Nottingham Forest, the creative efforts to open "stores" came at the expense of keeping resources in a financially stable neighborhood while survivors like Will slept in their cars. As a result of this divergence in bonding social capital, residents without an abundance of resources turned to federal and state agencies for assistance, but without linking capital to connect them to those in authority positions, the general sentiment from residents was that the government bureaucracy was bloated and slow-moving.

Thus, Ethan's heroic actions along with the countless other acts of kindness from Texas Gulf Coast residents do not dismiss the fact that people were still hurting six, twelve, and even twenty months after Hurricane Harvey. Diane was exhausted. Her employer had not given her time off to evacuate, and by the time she returned to her neighborhood in mid-September she had used all of her vacation days. To a certain extent, Diane was lucky. Some people did not have vacation days at all—working a minimum-wage job or as an hourly worker—so time off due to evacuation simply meant no income. Like Raelynn, Diane struggled to manage the everyday responsibilities that existed before the disaster along with the burdens Hurricane Harvey left behind. The road to recovery was far from over.

Back in Austin, Charles and his team strategized about other ways they could assist moving forward. When Charles spoke with the pastoral staff of churches located in the disaster recovery area, he could hear the exhaustion in their voices. These staff members had listened to people whose faith was shaken and who struggled to understand why God could allow such pain and misery. Ministers tried to offer hope of a better future, but even they could not tell when brighter days would arrive. Charles knew that the Austin Disaster Recovery Network needed to help not only the residents of Port Arthur, but also the churches in the area that people would turn to for support. "We've got to help them [the churches] take care of themselves so that they can help their communities," Charles said. "This is a marathon, not a short race."

Charles's marathon metaphor was right in one sense. Disaster recovery is long, arduous, and painful, just like a marathon. However, unlike a race where there is a start and a finish, resilience is a never-ending process. When a marathoner crosses the finish line, the heavy breathing will eventually slow, the sweating will subside, the pain will cease, and the body will return to how it was before the runner started their race. But for disaster survivors and communities seeking to build resilience, the trauma they experienced will fundamentally transform them, so much so that resilience is not about "bouncing back" but rather about "bouncing forward."[15] In the pages that follow, we want to explore those transformations—the adaptive and maladaptive ones. Here the marathon metaphor becomes even more problematic. If life in the moments before Harvey hit was a starting line, many of the residents we spoke to probably felt like they were running in reverse. Challenging mental health reactions coupled with physical health problems seemed to suggest life after Hurricane Harvey was worse than what it was before, with no improvement in sight. Others felt they had emerged stronger from the disaster. And as people shared their emotional, psychological, and physical transformations, they thought about preparing for the next disaster. Clearly, this was no marathon. Whether people were feeling stronger or weaker, Harvey had changed survivors in a way that made response and recovery more like a race that would go on forever.

6

After the Storm

August 25, 2018, came and went like any other late summer day—or, for that matter, like any other day in the current news environment. Texas news outlets like the *Houston Chronicle* sought to commemorate the one-year anniversary of Hurricane Harvey with front-page headlines that read "Coast Still in Harvey's Grip: From Rockport to Port Arthur, Life Revolves Around Storm." However, the majority of national news outlets, including the *New York Times*, gave little prominence to stories describing how Texas Gulf Coast residents were remembering the day that had consumed their lives for the past year.

The relative dearth of national media coverage on the one-year anniversary of Hurricane Harvey is not surprising. News outlets are more inclined to write about disasters when they are framed around the anniversary of the event rather than general disaster preparedness topics or collaborative efforts across different government agencies.[1] We don't doubt the lifespan of disaster news coverage tends to be much shorter when compared to other major news issues. Rather, research has shown the bulk of national news coverage concerning disasters happens within the first thirty days following the event.[2]

In the context of Hurricane Harvey, several other factors may have led news divisions to keep survivors' stories off the front pages of their papers and websites. Perhaps in the midst of a new hurricane season, recalling a 2017 disaster seemed like old news. Perhaps Hurricane Harvey was not scandalous enough. In a year with one scandal after another, from presidential payments to adult film stars to toddlers detained at the US–Mexico border, the intricacies of how and when disaster relief was allocated was perhaps just not newsworthy in comparison. Or maybe the most troubling interpretation from a community resilience perspective was that the lack of attention speaks to a cultural expectation we have placed on disaster recovery—that is, as a society, we may feel socially inclined to help disaster survivors in the immediate wake of a hurricane, but our "pull yourself up by your bootstraps" mentality leads us to believe the problems persisting one year later reflect a deficiency on the part of survivors rather than institutions or society at large. In her August 28 *New York Times* opinion column, longtime Houston resident Mimi Swartz summarized this sense of disinterest and "it's your problem, not mine" mentality when dealing with natural disasters:

> And yet that's what seems to be expected of us from the state and federal governments. So far, the state of Texas can't be bothered to help much with Harvey relief—Gov. Greg Abbott has refused to spend even a pittance from the state's nearly $12 billion rainy-day fund. And the Trump administration apparently believes that the $89 billion it set aside early this year for hurricane response is plenty to solve the problems of Texas, Florida and Puerto Rico combined. It looks to me like our much-touted individualism is about to be tested—and exploited—again . . . Maybe the flood—or the fire—hasn't come to your door yet. But think about this: Houston, still stranded by the lack of state and federal support, is already a model for future climate disasters.[3]

While national news outlets appeared to move on to the next news story, the fact remained that a year after Hurricane Harvey, many Texas Gulf Coast residents were still in pain. Questions lingered about whether these Texas communities were resilient enough to rebuild, recover, and move forward. When conversations like these happen outside of the broader public discourse, the perception might be that everything is fine and that the survivors and communities are resilient. If this is indeed the perception, it certainly does not match the reality that was reflected in our data.

The Texas Gulf Coast was vulnerable at each disaster phase of Hurricane Harvey. In the pre-event phase (chapter four), there were social and communicative cracks in resilience that existed long before Harvey made landfall, with implications for how residents would view their own personal risk and preparedness. As the event unfolded in the immediate days and weeks after the hurricane (chapter five), stories highlighted that bonding social capital had limits in helping survivors travel through their personal disaster purgatories. Here, in chapter six, we transition to the post-event phase and the efforts made for communities and their residents to be resilient and "bounce forward."[4] Certainly, resilience requires the ability to adapt and transform based on the stressors and challenges individuals and communities face.

Unfortunately, the individual mental, physical, and behavioral transformations that survivors talked about were rather negative (with a few exceptions) in the months following Harvey. Moreover, nonwhite and Latinx communities or those more socially and economically isolated struggled in different ways before and during the disaster, whereas the post-event phase revealed that nonwhite and economically disadvantaged individuals appeared more susceptible to complex mental and physical health challenges. Residents experienced a range of challenging mental health reactions that persisted well after the one-year anniversary of the hurricane. In fact, the Kaiser Family Foundation reported that more individuals believed their mental health had gotten worse when surveyed the year following Harvey than residents surveyed four months after the hurricane.

As residents slogged through this flood of emotions, they literally waded through germ-infested waters as well. The unsanitary post-disaster landscape coupled with the stress of displacement and recovery led to physical health problems. Even as individuals psychologically coped with Harvey's trauma, many believed they had grown from surviving the hurricane. However, this personal growth did not manifest itself into preparedness for the next time a disaster like Harvey would hit the Texas Gulf Coast.

To help make sense of this enduring emotional toll, we will take a look at the disaster mental health reactions following Hurricane Harvey and the racial, economic, and displacement factors that may have contributed to an increase in post-traumatic stress symptoms. Through the experiences of two of our "narrators," Stacey and Katie, we will hear how citizen volunteer efforts were not sufficient to fully address disaster mental health challenges. We then examine the differences in physical health problems based on survivors' displacement paths by sharing the stories of hotel living and the primarily Latinx Rose Wood Mobile Home Park. Finally, we shift focus from negative health transformations to a discussion of the more positive psychological and behavioral transformations residents made following Harvey.

In doing so, we consider if those changes will help make all the residents of coastal communities more resilient in the future.

A Toll on Mental Health

Exposure to a traumatic event can lead to a range of post-traumatic stress symptoms, such as flashbacks or intrusive thoughts. If a person directly experiences an event, knows someone directly impacted by an event, or repeatedly sees or hears details about the event, symptoms are often present. Ultimately, the frequency and severity of these symptoms may negatively impact a person's ability to function both professionally and personally. As a baseline reference point, it is projected that nearly 9 percent of US residents will receive a post-traumatic stress disorder (PTSD) diagnosis in their lifetime. This percentage is somewhat higher for women and nonwhite individuals[5]; however, the likelihood of experiencing PTSD symptoms jumps significantly after surviving a disaster.

The degree to which one is exposed to a disaster also influences the likelihood of receiving a PTSD diagnosis. Individuals may be indirectly exposed to a disaster by watching events unfold on television or by living in a different community but knowing someone directly impacted by a disaster. Conversely, individuals can be directly exposed by experiencing a range of stressors because of the disaster, such as having a home destroyed or getting injured. Study after study has found that more than one-third of individuals directly exposed to a disaster will likely meet all the necessary requirements for a PTSD diagnosis.[6] In contrast, the prevalence of PTSD is much lower for first responders (10 to 20 percent) and the overall population where the disaster occurred (5 to 10 percent).

Beyond exposure to the event, disaster mental health reactions may also differ depending on one's gender, race, and prior disaster exposure. According to the American Psychological Association's report on PTSD, women and people who are nonwhite are more likely to experience disaster-related PTSD. Nevertheless, like many "racial effects," once social class and/or income is introduced, a new level of "effect" tends to emerge and the "racial effect" diminishes.[7] This by no means suggests the absence of such an effect, but rather that socioeconomic status creates a new intersection that provides both clarity and precision as to how we come to understand the implications of disasters on the mental health of diverse survivors. Just like research has found that low-income black residents are typically the ones in greatest need for targeted recovery assistance,[8] so too are these same subgroups the ones often at greatest risk to be impacted both physically and mentally by the aftereffects of traumatic storms like Hurricane Harvey. As we would expect, that heightened risk for ill effects comes as much from where they live as it does from who they are. Chakraborty and colleagues report significant environmental and infrastructural inequities across neighborhoods in the Houston metropolitan area as a result of flooding during Hurricane Harvey.[9] They provide clear evidence to the dramatic differences the flooding had across racial and ethnic lines, suggesting an environmental injustice that exists in terms not only of housing and neighborhood infrastructure, but also of disproportionate health impact of the disaster among racial and ethnic groups. Susceptibility to the trauma and tragedy does in fact vary across racial and ethnic lines, but it is more likely to be exacerbated and devastating to diverse groups of residents who live in neighborhoods that were destroyed and now have few options as they wait for those places to be put back together.

Additionally, in terms of prior disaster exposure, it is possible that individuals living in disaster-prone areas may build up a certain degree of immunity to disaster-related stress. Just like a vaccine exposes individuals to a weakened form of a virus in order to increase antibodies to fight a disease, repeated exposure to hurricanes may provide residents with coping mechanisms. These proverbial antibodies may translate into developing preparatory strategies to reduce potential damages, recognizing the need to receive help in the immediate aftermath, or having the ability to think about the disaster in positive and constructive ways following the event.

In February 2019, Chambers, Fort Bend, Harris, Montgomery, and Victoria Counties, as well as the Houston Health Department, the Environmental Defense Fund, and Rice University, offered one of the first researched glimpses into Hurricane Harvey's mental health impact. This collaboration of public health departments, research institutions, and advocacy organizations launched the Hurricane Harvey Registry to better understand the mental health symptoms of nearly ten thousand Texas Gulf Coast residents. Over half of the registrants reported intrusive thoughts as the symptom they experienced most often, with

59 percent indicating that they "thought about it [Hurricane Harvey] when I didn't mean to" either "sometimes" or "often."[10]

Our work adds to the Children's Environmental Health Initiative (CEHI) initial findings by moving beyond individual symptoms and toward understanding the distribution of PTSD symptomatology across the Texas Gulf Coast in the first few months after Hurricane Harvey. Specifically, in the survey we distributed to the Texas Gulf Coast between October 2017 and early January 2018, residents indicated how distressed they were out of the post-traumatic stress symptoms listed in the Impact of Events Scale-Revised.[11] Because we surveyed people over a period of three months, our data can only provide a snapshot of PTSD epidemiology in the early part of the post-event phase. However, we can provide two time points (four months and one year) for mental health reactions from the Kaiser Family Foundation surveys.

Disaster mental health reactions can range from survivors experiencing a few or relatively mild post-traumatic stress symptoms to survivors experiencing symptoms that rise to the severity of meeting all the necessary criteria needed for a PTSD diagnosis. We examined both how distressed people rated their symptoms and whether those symptoms met the criterion for a PTSD diagnosis. In some cases, certain demographic groups were significantly more likely to meet the criterion for a PTSD diagnosis. In other cases, certain demographic groups were more likely to experience distressing post-traumatic stress symptoms, but that data did not lead to significant differences when probable PTSD was tested. Overall, slightly over a quarter of the people in our sample said they experienced enough stress to likely qualify for a probable PTSD diagnosis. In particular, race, access to post-disaster resources, type of displacement path, sex, and prior disaster exposure were all factors related to higher reporting of post-traumatic stress symptoms.

Factors Associated with Disaster Mental Health

First, when examining what factors were associated with mental health, we discovered some disparity across different racial groups. In general, nonwhite and Latinx residents experienced significantly more distressing post-traumatic stress symptoms than white residents. However, when we considered the diagnosis cutoff for meeting the criterion for a PTSD diagnosis, the difference between white and nonwhite residents was not as significant. A larger portion of nonwhite individuals still qualified for probable PTSD compared to white residents, but by a closer ratio. One-third of nonwhite individuals (34.1 percent) reported probable PTSD, whereas slightly less than one-quarter of white individuals (23.5 percent) reported a similar diagnosis. In terms of ethnicity, Latinx residents were more likely to qualify for PTSD than non-Latinx residents.

One could certainly speculate that these racial and ethnic differences in mental health reactions were due, in part, to both a lack of resources and the type of displacement path that compounded stress following Hurricane Harvey. Regardless of race, people who indicated being food insecure or having problems getting clothes, finding a place to stay and sleep, and getting clean were significantly more likely to have met the criterion for a PTSD diagnosis. Moreover, Texas Gulf Coast residents who either were forced or made the decision to evacuate reported more psychological distress than residents who sheltered-in-place, which supports preliminary work that examined disaster mental health after Hurricane Harvey.[12] Nonwhite residents reported the most distressing PTSD symptoms when staying at a hotel/motel, whereas, for white residents, the highest rates of stress were found among those who stayed with a friend or relative. Finally, Latinx residents who stayed in a shelter or were homeless experienced the highest rates of PTSD symptoms compared to other Latinx residents across different displacement paths.

On each of these fronts, nonwhite residents reported struggling to meet their basic needs more so than white residents. For example, two-thirds of nonwhites (66.7 percent) reported experiencing some degree of food insecurity compared to slightly more than half of whites (52.5 percent). Over three-fifths of nonwhite individuals (61.2 percent) were displaced following Harvey. In contrast, slightly over a third of white individuals (34.6 percent) were displaced. Nearly 90 percent of nonwhite individuals (88.5 percent) reported property damage, which was 25 percent higher than white individuals (64 percent).

Despite these disparities in mental health reactions that cut across race, resources, and displacement paths, CityLab, a media outlet that reports on urban issues of design, equity, and the environment, uncovered some discomforting bureaucratic and convoluted methods of disaster reimbursements to municipalities. Their October 2018 report suggested that disaster reimbursements appeared to benefit smaller, whiter towns more than predominately African American communities.[13] We argue the inequitable distribution of disaster relief resources may further compound the severity of mental health symptoms for communities that are predominately nonwhite.

Specifically, the Department of Housing and Urban Development's Community Development Block Grant funding was distributed through the Council of Government. This council is comprised of local representatives from several counties in the region. In southeastern Texas, the Council of Government for communities of large African American populations, like Beaumont and Port Arthur, was also the Council of Government for smaller, predominately white communities, like Taylor Landing. This Council of Government was organized in such a way that some of the smaller communities had disproportional influence over how funds were allocated. We would expect that a place like Port Arthur, where over 90 percent of residents were affected by Harvey and most happened to be nonwhite, would receive more federal dollars than Taylor Landing, where 10 percent of residents were impacted and mostly white. In reality, Taylor Landing received an estimated $60,000 of disaster funding per resident, while Port Arthur got crumbs in comparison—$84 per resident.[14]

At a societal level, this example captures the idea that those people in positions of power, influence, and privilege before a disaster are often the same ones in a position to control the purse strings after a disaster. At the individual level, this example reveals how policies have a human impact. On the surface, this CityLab report appears to address political and economic outcomes, but these reimbursements also have emotional and psychological consequences. For a Port Arthur resident—displaced, uncertain of what lay ahead, and hearing that their hometown was not getting the help it needed—the prospect of individual recovery may have seemed like a herculean, near-impossible task. In summary, the stresses of displacement, and food insecurity, and the baseline traumatic experience combined with the inequality of disaster relief, added challenges that may have contributed to the clear disparities in mental health reactions across racial groups.

Bucking Disaster Mental Health Trends

As much as our findings reflected what mental health providers and public health officials know about the distribution of disaster mental health reactions across a community, other findings contradicted previous work in this area. For instance, more men qualified for a likely PTSD diagnosis than women. Additionally, the inoculation hypothesis that suggests people with more prior disaster exposure actually suffer less challenging mental health reactions was not the case among our respondents. In fact, people who had experienced more traumas from previous disasters (i.e., property damage, perceived threat to life, loss of items with sentimental value) were more likely to report probable PTSD than residents who had not experienced as many disasters. This finding illuminates that Hurricane Harvey was not your typical disaster. Even though people like Beth, Larry, and Patty had experienced other disasters along the coast, they could not anticipate the volume of rain and the damage this disaster would cause in so many communities. Thus, any of the "antibodies" those coastal residents had previously built up were not enough to counter a newer, slower-moving version of a natural disaster like Hurricane Harvey.

Collectively, these findings reveal several social factors that may put disaster populations at risk for challenging mental health reactions. Nonwhite residents, those with fewer economic resources, and persons experiencing significant displacement remain populations needing assistance when it comes to disaster mental health resources. Moreover, slower-moving disasters are the new normal, and prior disaster exposure does not appear to inoculate against challenging mental health reactions. In turn, residents who have experienced previous hurricanes and were once thought to be less susceptible to challenging mental health reactions will also need support. Some of the support to address disaster mental health may come from professionals in a counseling setting, but it is also possible that survivors can access their social capital to alleviate distressing symptoms.

Social Capital and Disaster Mental Health

Surprisingly, we found that some aspects of social capital were associated with more psychological distress, whereas other components of social capital blunted that distress. For example, membership in community organizations was positively associated with psychological distress. Specifically, Texas Gulf Coast residents belonging to more community organizations were also likely to report more PTSD and depressive symptoms. Initially, these findings were unexpected, particularly given that nearly half of all survivors experiencing some type of structural damage expressed the need for more help. In addition, people were more effusive in praising the generosity of community members following Hurricane Harvey. After all, Charles from the Austin Disaster Recovery Network was worried that people felt forgotten. We thought that individuals fortunate enough to have connections to organizations would experience less challenging mental health reactions than residents who did not possess as much social capital. This assumption was based on the belief that individuals would then turn to the community organizations they belonged to for either material assistance or emotional support. We propose two potential explanations for this finding.

The first explanation is that residents may have used their membership in organizations less to find help for themselves following the disaster and more to become involved in helping other members of their community recover. One survivor turned to their church to help right away, explaining, "My local church went into action as soon as it was safe to be outside. We served meals, handed out clothing, and essential toiletries to families in need." Why did residents volunteer their time and effort after Hurricane Harvey? People volunteered because of a sense of duty, a connection to their community, and/or a defense mechanism of coping with what they had just experienced and were facing themselves. Perhaps keeping busy by helping others was a welcome distraction from the pieces of their lives that still needed to be picked up. Perhaps after having no control over Harvey's impact, residents believed they could regain some of that agency by choosing to help others. While this coping strategy served a palliative function, it may not have actually served to ameliorate challenging mental health reactions. Thus, by volunteering with multiple organizations, residents may have put other people's needs ahead of their own senses of well-being.

Another way of thinking about this potential explanation is to consider the "oxygen mask in the airplane" scenario. In the event of lost pressure in an airplane cabin, passengers are instructed to place their own oxygen masks on before assisting others. The rationale for this instruction is that one cannot fully help others if they themselves are in distress. This phenomenon has received a variety of names in the disaster literature, from compassion fatigue to vicarious trauma or secondary trauma, and the concept has traditionally been linked to professionals who work in trauma settings, such as social workers, therapists, and first responders. However, whether it is a mental health professional, an emergency management official, or an everyday citizen simply wanting to help a neighbor, anyone assuming a role that requires empathy may be exposing himself or herself to secondary trauma.[15]

Stacey, a young black professional, embodied this tension between offering help and needing support herself. When Stacey shared her story with us in July 2018, she admitted that she was "the kind of person that does better suppressing or avoiding certain overwhelming thoughts or unwanted feelings." In the immediate months following Harvey, she felt she could not escape visuals of others' pain and suffering, and this exposure led to both "sadness and depression." Stacey would turn off the local news coverage of Hurricane Harvey only to drive down roads along the Braes Bayou near her predominately Hispanic Houston neighborhood and watch other families less fortunate than her trying to salvage their homes. Stacey may not have viewed herself as a victim, but she witnessed the trauma of others on a daily basis. Even though Stacey turned to family and friends for support, she mentioned multiple times that she had "survivor's guilt or remorse mixed with favor that our homes or vehicles were not damaged."

Stacey searched for meaning in this tragedy and struggled to understand why she emerged with less damage than others. As part of this sense-making process, Stacey turned to the many organizations she belonged to. Like many other people we met, Stacey began to volunteer by donating to her local church. She also canvassed with the Houston Area Urban League in the primarily African American neighborhood of Kashmere Gardens. As part of this volunteer work, Stacey identified what Kashmere Gardens' residents needed as well as assessed whether their homes were safe to live in. Stacey busied herself with this volunteer work in hopes of suppressing her sadness and atoning for her crushing sense of guilt. In the short term, Stacey's connection to community organizations like her church and the Houston Area Urban League may have helped her cope, but Stacey also expressed that she had some post-traumatic stress symptoms (although probably not meeting the criterion for a PTSD diagnosis). Like nearly one in five residents (19.96 percent) expressed through the Kaiser Family Foundation one-year anniversary survey, Stacey still felt irritable and angry. She added that having thoughts about Hurricane Harvey made her "sad all over again."

Katie is another example of someone who put others' needs in front of her own. Katie was a Port Aransas resident who evacuated before the storm with little more than some clothes and a few family keepsakes. She returned to her neighborhood to find not only that her home was destroyed, but also that many of her belongings, including mementos from childhood, were no longer salvageable. Katie was having a hard time, and her mother, Marta (whom we met earlier), could tell. Nevertheless, Katie juggled her desire to help others with her own efforts to recover. Soon some volunteer organizations emerged, including a group of individuals in Port Aransas calling themselves "The Group to Bring the Marlins Home." This group decided to pool resources to rent twenty-six travel trailers for families who were displaced. Even though Katie was struggling with her own loss, she was one of those Port Aransas residents who got involved to make those travel trailers a reality.

We want to be clear that we cannot provide official diagnoses for Stacey or Katie, or any of our respondents. However, their stories do reflect previous research that suggests residents who have survived a disaster may experience some challenging mental health reactions even if the symptoms do not rise to a depression or PTSD diagnosis. We believe their stories are emblematic of how the impulse to help may have provided a temporary distraction from personal pain and anguish, but ultimately, involvement in an emergent volunteer group was not the panacea to the emotional stress after Harvey. Thus, some capacities conducive to building community resilience—such as social capital and civic engagement—may in fact represent a double-edged sword. Without question, the generosity and willingness of survivors could hasten the physical recovery efforts in a community. However, this help and support might also complicate individual disaster mental health reactions that could stall recovery on an entirely different level.

In addition to the vicarious trauma hypothesis, displacement paths may also help to better understand the relationship between involvement in community organizations and post-traumatic stress symptoms. We explored this association by further dividing our sample into those persons who were displaced and those who stayed in their communities. When we examined the relationship between involvement in community organizations and post-traumatic stress symptoms among displaced residents, the relationship was significant, meaning displaced residents who belonged to more community organizations were more likely to report post-traumatic stress symptoms than residents with strong community ties who did not evacuate. Why is this important? Well, we think this finding emphasizes the importance of place in addressing disaster mental health reactions. After Hurricane Harvey hit, social networks were partially fractured as many residents were uprooted from their communities. Those survivors who were displaced were no longer physically close to the organizations to which they belonged, and therefore, they were most likely unable to tap into their reservoir of social capital for emotional and material support. Whether it be a matter of vicarious trauma or an issue of displacement, the relationship between community organizations and post-traumatic stress symptoms reveals that natural disasters can impede some of the positive outcomes associated with active participation in the community and thus create a more complicated story than originally thought.

To some extent, involvement in community organizations seemed to be related to more challenging mental health reactions. Nevertheless, that didn't mean that other aspects of social capital—such as positive community perceptions or strong relationships with family, friends, and neighbors—were inherently detrimental to disaster mental health reactions. In fact, strong social ties and confidence in a community's ability to recover helped to alleviate post-traumatic stress and depression symptoms among survivors. Coastal residents who reported having a close companion, as well as having friends they saw on a regular basis, had less distressing depression symptoms. Further, residents who qualified for a probable PTSD diagnosis had significantly weaker social connections than residents who did not qualify. Our findings appear to confirm the importance of social support when it comes to disaster mental health.[16] Texas Gulf Coast residents were also more likely to experience less post-traumatic stress or depression if they believed their community had the capacity to grow, emerge stronger, and become better equipped for the next disaster that will certainly come along.

A Toll on Physical Health

In addition to challenging mental health reactions, survivors expressed a decline in their physical health in the months following Harvey. In fact, slightly over a quarter (26.8 percent) of the people we spoke with expressed concern for their health. Texas Gulf Coast residents responded to our survey roughly at the same time the Kaiser Family Foundation launched their initial round of data collection, and their results coincide with our findings. Four months following Hurricane Harvey, slightly over a quarter of respondents (25.4 percent) to the Kaiser survey described their overall health as "fair" or "poor." A year later, the Kaiser anniversary data revealed that residents were slightly more optimistic about their health, but nearly one in five residents (19.9 percent) still rated their overall health as "fair" or "poor."

In accordance with mental health, significant differences existed in survivors' physical health based on whether or not they were displaced. The Kaiser anniversary data revealed that over one-fifth of displaced residents (21.3 percent) indicated they or a family member had either experienced a new health condition or a current health condition had gotten worse since Hurricane Harvey. On the other hand, 12 percent of residents who did not evacuate indicated a new or worsening health condition since Harvey. Between the stories people shared with us and reports from the Hurricane Harvey Registry,[17] differences also existed in types of symptoms and health problems based on whether or not people evacuated or sheltered-in-place. People who stayed in their residence throughout the hurricane and cleanup phase reported more allergic reactions and respiratory issues, whereas residents staying in hotels feared that stress and poor eating habits led to weight gain.

According to the Hurricane Harvey Registry, the most common symptoms for those who stayed in their homes during the cleanup process were headaches, trouble breathing, and runny noses.[18] Given exposure to mold is often a problem following hurricanes, it is not surprising that those staying in their homes reported more allergies and respiratory problems. Even among our respondents, allergies ranked as one of the three main physical health issues cited. When asked about their health, one survivor responded, "I'm not sure if this has anything to do with the hurricane, but my allergies were a lot worse this year, and a lot of people I have spoken to have said the same." Another survivor was confident their allergies were due to Hurricane Harvey. The person commented, "I am naturally allergic to mold, not in a severe way but mildly. For a couple months afterward it was a little inconvenient."

Hurricane Harvey's physical toll on people stuck in flood-damaged homes was more than a "little inconvenient" for the predominately Latinx community of the Rose Wood Mobile Home Park located just north of Houston. The floodwaters left vehicles destroyed, mobile homes inundated with stagnant water, and residents trapped in a dank quagmire. Nearly every resident at the mobile park was a monolinguistic Spanish speaker, and severely limited in their options of where they could go. Therefore, many of the residents stayed in place. The late summer humidity was crushing—air-conditioning no longer worked, which only added to the nauseating feeling as the smell of sewage from the septic tanks lingered in the air. Just as Charles and his team at the ADRN saw an opportunity to help underserved communities following Harvey, the Houston nonprofit social service agency known as the Northwest Assistance Ministries sprang into action for Rose Wood.

When Northwest Assistance Ministries went into the community to assess how they could help, the volunteers discovered that by remaining in a flood-ravaged place, the Rose Wood residents exacerbated their health problems. Residents reported headaches and migraines, breathing problems, bronchitis, asthma, and skin allergies. While mobile homes and cars needed to be repaired so that residents could travel to work, the Northwest Assistance Ministries volunteers recognized that a more persistent problem existed. The living conditions for those forced to stay in their flood-ravaged homes were detrimental to survivors' physical health.

In contrast to those who sheltered-in-place, individuals who were displaced reported problems concentrating and skin rashes as their most common physical symptoms in the Hurricane Harvey Registry.[19] For most of the displaced who spoke with us, weight gain was the most cited physical health issue. In fact, weight gain seemed to be so prevalent a problem that the term "Harvey weight" entered the Texas Gulf Coast lexicon. Survivors gave two primary reasons for their weight gain. First, residents thought stress had led to health issues. Will, the African American resident who had recently moved to Houston and lived in his car after the hurricane, said he spent several days in the hospital in November 2017 with stomach issues because of the immense pressure he felt. Raelynn, the single mother who had trouble navigating FEMA paperwork, offered several causes for her weight gain, one of which was a lack of sleep. She was regularly up several times a night worrying about her future.

However, a majority of displaced residents blamed their increased waistlines on their living conditions. Residents who were displaced to hotels and motels lacked kitchen space to cook meals. Without a kitchen, Juanita turned to fast food to fuel her recovery. She longed for a home-cooked meal. As if mentally checking things off a wish list, Juanita expressed, "If I could just cook one meal . . ." She imagined her road to recovery might be better if she had access to a kitchen. Compounding the stress of motel living, Juanita learned shortly after Hurricane Harvey that she was pre-diabetic and needed medication. Raelynn and Beth also blamed fast food for their weight gain. As Beth said, "Living in the hotel was helpful but good nutrition was a challenge." Even when Beth was able to move back into the upstairs of her house, she believed the anxiety of getting their lives back to a normal routine had led her family to unhealthy comfort foods.

The Bright Side of Disaster Recovery

Despite coping with challenging mental health reactions and experiencing a spike in allergies and other physical health symptoms, several of the residents also expressed elements of post-traumatic growth, which refers to "positive psychological change" following a traumatic event like a natural disaster.[20] Hurricane Harvey created an opening that allowed some individuals to see themselves, their relationships, or even their futures in a new light. As residents made sense of what happened to them in late August 2017, they restructured their traumatic experiences to find the good that derives from horrible circumstances. It is not uncommon for individuals who have gone through a trauma to experience challenging mental health reactions like post-traumatic stress symptoms while simultaneously disclosing that they have made positive changes in their lives.[21] People can experience post-traumatic growth through a deeper appreciation for life, stronger spirituality, stronger self-concept, deeper interpersonal relationships, and a renewed sense of purpose.[22] Survivors offered examples that illustrated each element of post-traumatic growth.

Most often, people referenced a deeper appreciation for life. Residents said that Harvey "put things into perspective" and helped them "not to sweat the small stuff." Even though people were willing to share the challenges they were still facing in moving back into their neighborhoods or repairing their homes, they often qualified those struggles by saying they felt blessed and acknowledging other people in greater need. By recognizing the plight of others, survivors seemed to appreciate what they still had even if Harvey had taken so much from them already. Beth was certainly more appreciative of the blessings in her life. Even though she expressed admiration for her tight-knit neighborhood, she was in no mood to hear others' perpetual complaints about the recovery process. While Beth did not know the central argument of our book, she saw firsthand that while her "life is less perfect" after Hurricane Harvey, her disaster experience was drastically different when compared to communities of color and the socially and economically disadvantaged. As Beth said, "We are a white, middle-class community living in good-quality housing and have health insurance. We had the option to buy flood insurance and many of us had done so. We are not worrying where the next meal is coming from and we all have roofs over our heads."

Given the pivotal role places of worship and other faith-based groups played in Hurricane Harvey's immediate wake, as well as residents' connection to religion prior to the disaster, it came as no surprise that people would reference a stronger spiritual life as a form of growth during their disaster recovery experience. From what people told us and because of the high degree of religiosity that already existed in the Texas Gulf Coast before Harvey, it is unclear whether Texas Gulf Coast residents actually developed a deeper spiritual relationship. Rather, survivors' stories seem to suggest that Hurricane Harvey reinforced their strong spiritual ties. For instance, instead of expressing anger at God or questioning why this level of suffering had to take place, one survivor said that their faith in God was one of the only constants in this turbulent time. For this survivor, her life may be forever demarcated into life before Harvey and life after Harvey, but nevertheless, she said, "I still trust God with my life."

The survivors also found an inner strength they did not know they had prior to Hurricane Harvey. As one person put it, "We didn't know how strong we were until Hurricane Harvey came. We can deal with a lot." Juanita, a Port Arthur resident, expressed a similar sentiment. Like most of the people whose stories we shared in earlier chapters, Juanita did not expect Harvey to be as destructive as it was. Emerging on the other side of the hurricane, Juanita was thankful she had survived given that she was completely unprepared. She credited her survival to her inner, faith-driven strength. When we spoke with Juanita, she was still living in a motel and dealing with all the inconveniences that come with living in a confined space. Nevertheless, she said, "When you have something to live for and people that are counting on you, you don't give up . . . I just look forward to a brighter day. It is hard, but the storm didn't take me, so I won't let this either."

Hurricane Harvey also helped residents develop deeper, more meaningful relationships with their family, friends, and neighbors. Many people turned to family and friends for material and emotional support. As residents evacuated and were dispersed to shelters and hotels, those who were either left behind or had already returned to their neighborhoods felt their absence. Patty thought her family's recovery was going well, but the thing she missed the most was her neighbors. As she put it, "I need my girlfriends back." In Beth's neighborhood, which was once bustling with backyard barbeques and moms' club meetings, the displacement was certainly felt and the neighbors were clearly missed. "There has been a strange quietness about the place," Beth said. "Far fewer children playing, dogs being walked, runners and walkers." But amid the stillness and brimming anticipation of displaced neighbors returning, new friendships emerged. Some of Beth's neighbors had just been familiar faces that she would see as she ran errands or attended neighborhood gatherings. Now, she got to really know them on a deeper, more meaningful level. As one survivor said, "Neighbors who did not do more than wave to each other now tend to talk one-on-one more often." Another survivor echoed this sentiment, saying, "We know our neighbors better now, so that's good."

New and more meaningful relationships were forged through a shared commonality. As one survivor said, "It brought people closer together. And we have a bond that is unique that will stand the test of time due to getting through the disaster together." This was certainly the case for Raelynn. After Hurricane Harvey, Raelynn found her daughter's school to be a great resource for both material and social support. The school offered volunteers and supplies to help people clean up and remove debris from homes. In addition, counselors were on-site to help not only children but also parents. With her stress level rising as she tried to find a second job to cover the expenses incurred after the disaster, Raelynn attended three counseling sessions at the school. She also turned to her priest for spiritual guidance. As she reflected on how her community had changed since Harvey, Raelynn referenced how those connections at church and her daughter's school changed her idea of community: "During the flood, I feel like it made us closer, because we lived through uncertain times together, through a flood . . . I now feel a bit closer to my daughter's school, our community, and our church. I feel I have expanded my community."

Finally, multiple people expressed a renewed sense of purpose. After surviving one of the most devastating hurricanes in US history, witnessing the generosity of neighbors, and recognizing that they were unprepared for Harvey, residents resolved to become more involved in the life of their communities. In some instances, this involvement amounted to joining community organizations. In other cases, residents committed to helping their neighbors prepare for future disasters.

When the Next Hurricane Strikes . . .

Disaster phases are cyclical. The post-event phase is often characterized as the months following the disaster when community members rebuild, businesses reopen, and people transition from trying to survive the initial shock to coping with the emotional trauma they experienced. Eventually, though, disaster survivors move beyond addressing issues from the most recent disaster to anticipating the next disaster. At this point, the boundary between the post-event phase and the pre-event phase becomes fluid as residents draw on their most recent experience to plan for and possibly mitigate the impact of future disasters. We spoke with survivors at this intersection between post-event and a new pre-event. As we combed through our data and the conversations we had with people along the Texas Gulf Coast, thoughts toward hurricane risk and preparedness were mixed. Some people were skeptical about the risk factors that exacerbated Harvey's impact. Others were adamant that they needed to be more self-reliant and have a plan for the next hurricane. The differences in these views may be due in part to individuals' displacement paths following Hurricane Harvey, their economic status, and their connections to the community.

In regard to displacement and its relationship to risk and preparedness, we wanted to ascertain whether residents perceived climate change as a threat to their economic, health, and environmental well-being. It was important to ask these questions because several studies since Hurricane Harvey have concluded that climate change heightened the intensity of the disaster. Specifically, atmospheric scientists claim abnormally higher temperatures in the Gulf of Mexico resulted in a greater volume of rain.[23] The amount of rain may be due in part to changes in atmospheric pressure, which slow down the wind and allow storms to stay in place for longer periods of time.[24] Further, scientists project that Harvey was not an anomaly. US residents living along the coasts can expect slower-moving storms in the future. Based on this evidence, Harvey was not simply another disaster. It was a climate change disaster.

The public's climate change risk perceptions matter. A great deal of research has found that disaster risk perception is often an important factor in whether or not individuals prepare for disasters. While Kim and Kang found a direct relationship between disaster risk perception and taking preparedness steps before and during a hurricane,[25] the relationship between disaster risk perception and preparedness is often more complicated and includes other variables that may mediate the relationship. For instance, those who think they are at greater risk of experiencing a disaster are more likely to seek out information on how to prepare, which in turn has led to individuals taking mitigation actions to reduce negative disaster consequences.[26] In other instances, the combination of higher disaster risk perception and other factors like efficacy[27] or personal responsibility[28] influence individual disaster preparedness. In the context of climate change, past research has revealed that people who survived a flood were more likely to see climate change as a threat, and in turn were more likely to support efforts to address climate change and its impact on weather-related disasters.[29] Thus, if self-reliance is emphasized in federal disaster management strategies and tacitly reinforced through US cultural views, people living in disaster-prone areas first need to identify and understand what puts themselves, their families, and their communities at risk before they can prepare for impending disasters.

However, when we talked to people along the coast, all of whom came from communities hit by this climate change disaster, differences emerged regarding whether or not climate change was viewed as threatening to their way of life. Displacement was a factor in these differing perceptions. Those who evacuated were significantly more likely to view climate change as a risk compared to those residents who were able to stay in their homes during Hurricane Harvey. Specifically, less than half of those residents who stayed at home agreed that climate change would impact them economically in the next twenty-five years. In contrast, more than 75 percent of those who were displaced to families' and friends' houses and nearly 60 percent of those who evacuated to shelters believed that climate change would dramatically chip away at their bank accounts. This pattern continued when we asked about climate change's risk to one's health. Again, less than half of those residents who did not evacuate felt like climate change would negatively impact their health, whereas nearly 60 percent of those displaced in some form believed that climate change would be detrimental to their overall physical well-being.

Based on these results, Hurricane Harvey made climate change more realistic and top-of-mind for those directly impacted by the disaster. Climate change was no longer some complex scientific concept or some issue bandied about by politicians; instead, it became emotional and economic. Climate change was now associated with living in crowded, noisy shelters or returning to thousands of dollars in damages. Climate change seemed, at least for some, to be a reasonable explanation for the super-storm they just experienced.

According to the one-year anniversary data from the Kaiser Family Foundation,[30] displacement had an impact beyond risk perception. Residents whose families evacuated their homes for any amount of time were significantly more likely to have taken disaster preparedness actions for the upcoming hurricane season when compared with residents who stayed in their homes during Hurricane Harvey. Displacement certainly had an impact on Linda, the Latina resident whose family evacuated by boat from their first-floor apartment. One year later, Linda was still searching for a new place to live. She felt her landlord had left her with no instruction on what to do when the hurricane hit, where to turn for help, and when to evacuate. Linda's terrifying experience toggling back and forth between televised weather reports in a foreign language and the creeping floodwaters outside her window persuaded her to become more informed about disaster preparedness. She explained, "Personally, now I do more research about the weather every time I go out. I have learned about the map of flood risk areas, which I will take into account when I look for a new place to live." Likewise, Diane, who was also displaced and hopped from one hotel to the next, took preparedness actions. Diane's friend had been the one to email her with the directive to evacuate. Having heeded that advice, Diane wanted to make sure other people in her neighborhood might also benefit from disaster-related communication among friends in the future. When we spoke with Diane, she was working to create a communication infrastructure to check in on senior neighbors and ensure they received proper warnings. Diane added, "I know there are some neighbors who don't use Internet or text, and someone needs to cover for these offline neighbors."

In addition to displacement as a factor for disaster preparedness, economic status contributed to whether or not families prepared and what actions they took. Preparedness actions run along a financial continuum from no expense (e.g., talking about what to do in case a disaster happens) to relatively minor expenses (e.g., creating a disaster kit) to major expenses (e.g., home renovations to make structures resilient to wind and flood damage).

According to the Kaiser Family Foundation anniversary survey, the most common preparedness actions taken were located on the little-to-no-expense end of the spectrum. Over three-quarters (76.5 percent) of residents surveyed by the Kaiser Family Foundation had compiled a home disaster kit with materials that could last them several days in an emergency. Like Linda and Diane, nearly two-thirds (63.1 percent) of residents had created a family disaster communication plan. In contrast, less than one in five residents had purchased additional insurance

(18.4 percent), and a third of residents (33.7 percent) had made renovations to make their homes resilient to structural damage. When we dove into the Kaiser Family Foundation anniversary data, we saw that those with lower incomes were financially constrained to take preparedness actions. Specifically, roughly four in ten families (41.4 percent) below the US federal poverty line had taken preparedness actions, whereas above the US federal poverty line, five in ten families (49.7 percent) had prepared.

Finally, social capital was a potential factor that encouraged preparedness. During our conversations, residents hoped their individual actions to prepare for future disasters would reverberate to collective disaster management efforts in their communities. Multiple people we interviewed expressed an interest in joining preexisting community outreach and volunteer programs.

As the residents in Nottingham Forest developed a communication plan that would ensure everyone in the subdivision had information to prepare for, respond to, and recover from a future disaster, Diane also wanted to take the opportunity to advocate for her neighborhood. Like Alice and Beth, Diane was caught off guard by the release of the Addicks and Barker reservoirs. After the rain stopped, residents thought that they had survived the worst of the damage—only to see their homes flooded as the water from the reservoirs flowed into their neighborhoods. The initial shock turned to anger as reports surfaced that the US Army Corps of Engineers knew the reservoirs would need to be released but did not warn the public well enough in advance. Diane was frustrated by both the lack of transparency and perceived disregard for the best interests of her neighborhood. In turn, Diane wanted to channel that anger into community engagement. She mentioned, "Our neighborhood will join other neighborhoods to fight for funding to prevent another reservoir release type of flooding." Like the Nottingham Forest "stores," where neighbors could walk into living rooms and pick up food and other supplies that were donated, the upper-middle-class subdivision of Nottingham Forest, yet again, was an exemplar of how neighborhoods with high bonding social capital were able to organize to improve the well-being of the people in their proximate social networks.

On the whole, data reveal that Hurricane Harvey spurred some individuals and neighborhoods to become resilient to future disasters;

however, the findings may also be a harbinger that the Texas Gulf Coast will become a patchwork of preparedness, where displacement, economic status, and a neighborhood's location will determine whether or not a citizen is ready for the next hurricane.

Nottingham Forest had the trifecta of factors that influenced risk and preparedness. Neighbors were displaced, but many families had the means and connections to help one another and advocate for themselves at the municipal level. But the Nottingham Forest story stands in stark contrast to that of Linda, who didn't have the bonding social capital to organize with a group of neighbors or the linking social capital to reach policymakers. Instead, months after being displaced, she was still looking for a place to live and was limited to individual preparedness actions, such as trying to make sense of floodplains. She could not afford a new chain for her son's bike, so it is possible compiling the items for a home disaster kit may have been too costly of an expense.

Certainly, the people of the mobile home park did not share the same capacity to prepare as Diane and her friends did. Many of these Spanish-speaking residents were linguistically isolated. Some were undocumented and any efforts to seek government support may have drawn unwanted attention to their immigration status. Ultimately, these findings across different research teams raise the question of whether the federal government endorsement of Whole Community disaster management is effectively addressing the *whole community*. It is a question that city councils, emergency management, public health officials, and academics are currently grappling with answering.

Pockets of Conversation

The first anniversary of Hurricane Harvey may not have garnered the national media attention it deserved. People were still in mental, emotional, and physical pain. People were still recovering. And *some* were preparing for future hurricanes. All were doing so with quiet dignity and stories that deserved to be told at the one-year mark. However, the relative national silence about Hurricane Harvey's one-year anniversary should not be misconstrued for silence altogether. Pockets of conversations have been taking place among public health officials, emergency managers, and academics. For instance, on the eve of the one-year anniversary, the Robert Wood Johnson Foundation blogged about lessons learned from a public health perspective. A couple days later, the University of Texas at Austin hosted a Harvey Research Symposium in Port Aransas. These pockets of conversation among practitioners and academics are sorely needed.

In the pages that follow, we contribute to this conversation by outlining a citizen-centered agenda to build community resilience. Any conversation about how to strengthen communities before, during, and after disasters must include all sectors of the community, including the everyday citizens whose stories we have shared throughout this book. The everyday citizen is the most important resource in building resilient communities. Unfortunately, citizens are disempowered to participate in making their communities stronger when the places they live have cracks in resilience, are mired in disaster purgatories, and are patchworks of preparedness. Across different data points, from our interviews to the Kaiser Family Foundation survey, it is clear that communities of color, the socially isolated, and the economically disadvantaged are the ones that fall through those cracks, feel stuck in disaster purgatories, and are stranded in the spaces they occupy—unprepared. A citizen-centered agenda proposes a range of interventions at the individual, organizational, and community levels to ensure that conversations about resilience generate actions that empower all residents—from Beth and Diane to Stacey and Will, and to all the people in between who have or will eventually have a disaster story to tell.

7

Changes

It was not Washington's finest hour. For months, Capitol Hill and the White House stood at an impasse over a disaster aid bill that would provide comprehensive relief to citizens in need. The spring 2019 floods devastated midwestern farmers. Puerto Ricans still reeled from Hurricane Maria. California residents, whose homes were scorched by the 2018 wildfires, patiently waited for help. Included in this $19 billion aid package was $4 billion earmarked for relief to Hurricane Harvey survivors. In 2018, previous legislation had granted Texas this funding for both recovery and mitigation efforts. However, a year had passed, and the US Department of Housing and Urban Development, along with the Office of Management and Budget, had not provided guidelines on accessing those funds, meaning the state could not spend the $4 billion. To expedite the use of Harvey funds, Texas Senator John Cornyn inserted language into the bill that would release the $4 billion originally promised in 2018 to the state of Texas within ninety days after the bill was signed into law.[1] Despite a Texas congressman's procedural maneuvers to stall the legislation in the House of Representatives, the bill eventually passed both chambers of Congress with large bipartisan majorities. President Trump relented to his request for border wall funding and signed the bill into law in early June.[2]

For a bill that affected all areas of the country and would benefit the constituents of Republican and Democratic leaders alike, gridlock and the inability to help disaster survivors at their most vulnerable time overshadowed the bipartisan final vote total and prolonged the suffering of disaster survivors. Instead of helping survivors with a step in the right direction, this episode illustrated once again one of the basic assumptions of Whole Community disaster management: that total reliance on the US federal government to protect and assist disaster-impacted communities is not sustainable.[3] Failure of the federal government to efficiently and effectively intervene in disaster planning, response, and recovery comes at a time when the frequency and magnitude of disasters is increasing. When President Trump signed the aid bill into law, the US had experienced twenty-two "billion-dollar disasters" since Hurricane Harvey.[4] Solutions are needed if the US is going to address this growing threat. Our research suggests that federal, state, and municipal governments must involve citizens in the process to build resilience in communities or we stand to repeat the disaster response and recovery cycle that continues to reflect a fractured policy.

The months-long struggle to pass disaster aid may not have been Washington's finest hour, but there were countless hours wherein survivors exemplified the best in civic responsibility and action. New challenges emerged at each phase of Hurricane Harvey that tested the resilience of Texas Gulf Coast residents, but even in the midst of tumultuous change, the goodness of disaster survivors remained constant. Indeed, the everyday citizen was the greatest capacity these coastal communities had toward recovering and building resilience.

It is worth noting we use the term *citizen* to refer to all people, including the immigrants along the southern US border who may or may not ever claim any official citizenship status, but who were without question a part of and contributed to helping others through this collectively shared experience. Citizens can be resources and as such possess community relationships and resilience attributes like flexibility, creativity, efficacy, diversity, and social justice.[5]

We found countless examples in the stories that people told us. We saw flexibility in Ethan's quick thinking as he grabbed his kayak to rescue neighbors. We found elements of creativity in the pop-up neighborhood "stores" that appeared in Beth's subdivision. We got a sense of the collective efficacy that drove Diane and her friends to establish better communication with the city. We heard the deep commitment to social justice that inspired strangers like Charles and Stacey to help residents who were neglected and needed more help than they did. We listened to the resolve that Beth communicated clearly in the weeks after losing a lot but was not willing to give up.

As we discussed earlier, a key principle to the Whole Community disaster management approach is to strengthen what works well in individual communities—fitting preparedness, response, and recovery into the DNA of the community. If the everyday citizen is the greatest capacity for community resilience, then interventions must address how citizens can unleash their full potential to usher their communities through crisis. By highlighting this community strength, citizens can be part of the solution to fix the cracks in resilience, to shorten disaster purgatories, and to sew together the patchworks of preparedness highlighted throughout the previous chapters.

As part of a citizen-centered disaster agenda, we propose using an ecological framework that focuses on the actions that individuals, organizations, communities, and nations as a whole can take to bring out the best in its citizens before, during, and after disasters. These multilevel interventions may come in the form of informal conversations that require no expense, or in the form of events and programs implemented by organizations deeply connected to their local communities. Interventions may be policies that not only require economic investments, but also a significant shift in how we address disaster management as a society. Interventions may be independent of other coordinated efforts to build resilience, but the ecological framework proposes that interventions are typically most successful when efforts are implemented at each individual level of aggregation,[6] from the neighborhood (micro-level) to the nation (macro-level).

An ecological framework—used to help us better understand disaster intervention—reinforces the importance of place by acknowledging that individuals are not solely responsible for their ability to respond and cope across all disaster phases. A variety of social and economic factors influence how people respond to disasters. In fact, Sallis and colleagues argue that an ecological approach can "enhance human dignity by moving beyond explanations that hold individuals responsible for, and even blame them for, harmful behaviors."[7] Instead, an ecological approach helps to transform places into an environment that supports citizens and provides them with multiple avenues to engage in particular behaviors, which for the purposes of this book include preparing for, responding to, and recovering from natural disasters. We begin by reviewing the interventions easiest to implement, which occur at the interpersonal level between neighbors, before considering the more complicated organizational, community, and federal interventions.

At the Interpersonal Level: Citizen Disaster Communication

Everyday citizens can implement interpersonal disaster interventions through the taken-for-granted neighborly activities they engage in every day. After speaking with many Harvey survivors, we learned that the ordinary actions of just talking with neighbors, belonging to community organizations, and attending church or engaging with a spiritual community were existing strengths that should be emphasized to help individuals better prepare for future disasters. Survivors may not have realized at the time that these types of daily activities had the capacity to build resilience; they just needed a change in perspective.

The high level of informal connection and the interactions neighbors had with one another were taken-for-granted strengths that could be used to engage in citizen disaster communication.[8] This type of communication refers to the sharing of information and stories with family, friends, and neighbors to help them prepare for and respond more appropriately to disasters. Before a disaster, citizen disaster communication may include residents talking with fellow neighbors about the possibility of experiencing a disaster or what steps they could take to protect their homes. Maybe the conversation needs to be about saving important documents, or what the necessary steps are, or what agencies to talk with about the purchase of disaster insurance. When a disaster strikes, individuals need to develop a way to communicate with one another to make sure that rumors are not spread. They also need to know how best to connect with people to see if they are okay and to confirm the legitimacy of reports about the disaster.

In Beth's case, she doesn't have to radically change her social life in order to be a disaster citizen. In fact, her social life provides her the opportunity to model for others what it means to be a disaster citizen. Beth simply needs to incorporate conversations about preparedness into those backyard barbeques and moms' club meetings. It could be something as simple as asking a neighbor if they are planning on putting together a home disaster kit or explaining to a neighbor the importance of purchasing flood insurance and who she used as her insurance provider. We don't want to oversimplify the process of preparedness, but we see how cities are so hyper-focused on the big-picture preparedness plans that they sometimes overlook the critical role that individuals can play in helping to build and sustain community resilience.

Citizen disaster communication can also yield positive outcomes in the post-event phase of a natural disaster. Multiple studies have found that the more citizens share their disaster experiences with one another, the more likely residents perceive their community as resilient.[9] Moreover, citizen disaster communication may help to facilitate positive mental health reactions following a disaster. For example, after Hurricane Matthew in 2016, residents who talked more frequently about how to help their community recover were more likely to report feelings of post-traumatic growth compared to those who talked little about community recovery.[10] These findings illustrate that disaster-focused conversations between neighbors could help to reinforce the strong feelings of belonging that already existed along the Texas Gulf Coast. These conversations can also help to bolster individual growth in communities, where over a quarter of the people we interviewed qualified for probable PTSD in the immediate months following Hurricane Harvey.

Ultimately, citizen disaster communication is a relatively easy intervention to develop and implement as a complement to coping mechanisms that span disaster phases. In several of the stories we heard, residents were already engaging in some of those citizen disaster communication processes. In other instances, neighbors were talking about disasters but perhaps encouraging maladaptive coping behaviors, such as when Beth and her neighbors were joking about Harvey's impact or when Raelynn heard comments that might discourage someone from applying for federal assistance. Or in other situations, neighbors interacted frequently with one another, but the content of the conversations never focused on disaster planning, response, and recovery. The latter two scenarios illustrate the importance of developing more formal efforts emanating from official sources of information that could accompany efforts to promote citizen disaster communication. Specifically, civic organizations and local government agencies need to develop and offer the tools and resources to help residents talk about disasters in productive ways with their neighbors. In the following section, we identify organizational and community interventions that may help to empower residents in the building of community resilience.

At the Organizational and Community Levels:
Hearing from the People

Organizational and community-based interventions may include engaging the public in discussions of disaster risk and planning, hosting preparedness programs and events through established organizations, and incentivizing translocal ties through regional time banking or community currencies. To begin, a visible crack in resilience that existed before Hurricane Harvey was a perceived lack of communication between the public and community disaster management teams. Nearly half of all the people we spoke with did not believe their community tried to prevent or prepare for impending disasters.

Furthermore, Latinx residents were significantly more likely to hold a negative view of their community's disaster communication compared to non-Latinx residents. Even if municipal governments had emergency plans in place, this finding implies that the average citizen was not invited to, involved with, or invested in their community's disaster management planning. Additionally, the perceived ineffective communication between local governments and the Latinx population confirms the work of the Houston Immigration Legal Services Collaborative (HILSC), which found that mistrust, language barriers, and a lack of attention to literacy levels compounded the response and recovery challenges for immigrant and Latinx communities. These communication failures were also illustrated in the stories people shared with us. If communities had talked with Linda, who struggled to access and process hurricane warnings because of the significant language barrier, they may have been able to create alternative messages that would have helped her better understand what was happening, and when to evacuate. If communities had sought the opinions of young, middle-class families like Claire's, they might have known that people who were living outside of the floodplain assumed they were protected from catastrophic flooding, and consequently would not feel the need to purchase any type of flood insurance.

Communication failures between formal disaster management organizations and the public are not new developments. Emergency management officials often make efforts to be inclusive of diverse audiences but fall short of the comprehensive approach that is needed in order to address this diversity. For example, the Houston Department of Emergency Management offers information in a variety of languages. Nevertheless, simple dissemination of preparedness information to the public is not enough.[11] As Dr. Umair Shah, who leads the Houston Department of Emergency Management, noted in a conversation with the Robert Wood Johnson Foundation, emergency management and public health groups cannot passively provide information and wait for the public to access services. Instead, emergency management and public health departments must engage the public, listen to their needs, and based on those needs, bring services to the residents.[12] Dr. Shah outlined a useful approach making four key points that are worth repeating.

Take Public Health to the Public

Instead of assuming that people can access services in an often challenged and broken down public transit system after a natural disaster, make plans to take services and supplies to them. This may mean developing alternative exit strategies for homeless and low-income residents of flood threatened neighborhoods. It may also mean that cities will need to consider developing a plan for mobile outreach in those locations that are cut off, hard to reach, or comprised primarily of place-bound groups with few local services. The Houston public health team created "Health Villages," which were retrofitted RVs designed to provide basic services like vaccines and supplies for pets, food, cleaning supplies, and even basic strategies for cleaning up after a disaster. This strategy was about taking the solution to the public and not waiting for them to show up at some predetermined site to receive care that many people could neither access nor find.

Communicate and Engage

It is important that we rely heavily on social media and other public communication outlets (YouTube, Twitter, Facebook, etc.) to provide information access for populations that are being threatened by a disaster or experiencing its consequences firsthand. Groups need to be updated constantly regarding opportunities, issues of safety, strategies for response, and calls for assistance. Corporations, faith communities, local and regional service providers, individual citizens, and various other actors can be important in filling the information gap that can reach a diverse, multicultural, multigenerational, heterogeneous population with a variety of needs throughout the Houston area and communities up and down the Texas Gulf Coast. Social media was important to Dr. Shah and his team in order to focus on immediate needs while at the same time raising the visibility of the impending public health crisis that was brewing in Harvey's aftermath. Dr. Shah recounted:

> It truly comes down to the three V's of public health. When you raise the visibility, you have a chance at demonstrating the value of your work. And once you show the value, the 3rd V kicks in: validation. Validation by folks wanting to invest in the work resource-wide or through pro-health policies. It has worked for our department and though we are talking about emergencies here, indeed we have learned the 3 V's go well beyond emergency response.[13]

We have a news cycle that never shuts off and sends constant updates and alerts to our phones and tablets via Facebook, Twitter, and even from direct news sources. Using these sources to share in tragedy and loss, as well as recovery and rebuilding, is vital to building and maintaining community resilience that necessarily requires partnership and collaboration.

It Takes a Village; Call on Partners

Dr. Shah reminded everyone that public health officials cannot handle disaster alone, though they often try. Developing and maintaining healthy partnerships across the service provider landscape appears to be integral to surviving disasters and coming out the other side stronger and better equipped for the next event. Hurricane Harvey was a response by all government and non-government entities that sometimes collectively looked like a well-oiled machine, and other times a machine that was broken down and in need of serious repair.

Be Resilient; Plan for the Unknown

Dr. Shah provided one last common-sense principle that might be of some help when considering what factors can be crucial to building any community's resilience. The history behind natural disasters in the United States suggests that patterns are important and preparation is key to survival and recovery. Communities cannot afford to be lax in their planning and preparation on the larger community level (city, county, metro area) or on the local neighborhood and citizen level. So many stories from survivors told of a newfound friendship or close bond that they developed with their neighbors in the face of the tragedy and the pain of recovery. Just as important are the efforts to sustain these types of relationships, which will go a long way in the preparation for the next storm or looming disaster.

At the Organizational and Community Levels: Incorporating the Citizens' Voice Into Resilience Efforts

In order to close the communication divide between emergency management professionals and the general public (particularly linguistically isolated populations), local governments, emergency management, and public health agencies must find a way to determine residents' communication needs prior to the development of city-wide disaster management and communication plans. Fortunately, an abundance of resources exists for communities to engage fellow citizens and recognize the unique needs of a diverse and socially complex community. The Communities Advancing Resilience Toolkit includes several assessments that engage a variety of stakeholders in identifying community strengths and weaknesses.[14] These assessments can be conducted in small groups and include activities like creating community ecological maps, conducting a SWOT analysis (strengths, weaknesses, opportunities, and threats), or completing a capacity and vulnerability assessment. For instance, a community ecological map, which evaluates the strength of the relationships and amount of interaction residents have with different organizations, may help to identify groups that could be trusted conduits where information can flow to particularly hard-to-reach populations.

In the context of Hurricane Harvey, one-fifth of respondents that participated in the Kaiser Family Foundation survey four months following the disaster expressed concern that seeking help during Harvey would draw unwanted attention to their or a family member's immigration status. An ecological map might have revealed these concerns before the disaster occurred if residents had identified law enforcement as a group with which they had limited interaction and whose relationship has been and continues to be stressful. In the short term, municipal leaders might want to consider identifying other officials who could act as important, trusted mediators and brokers of information sources for immigrant communities. Simultaneously, as part of a longer-term strategic plan, officials might consider developing an approach to foster a better relationship between law enforcement and immigrant communities. When a disaster strikes, immigrant populations need to feel comfortable seeking help from authorities instead of worried about what might happen if additional information about them is revealed or discovered.

Another approach that communities might consider in preparing and empowering its citizens in advance of the next natural disaster is the implementation of Photo Voice to engage local residents. Photo Voice is a form of participatory action research that provides cameras to often marginalized members of society and encourages them to document their lived experiences as well as community strengths and weaknesses.[15] Given that so many of the negative disaster consequences appeared to disproportionately affect low-income populations and people of color, the Photo Voice method, with its emphasis on working with marginalized populations, may be an appropriate way to foster participation among groups who tend to be the most vulnerable and marginalized during and even after disasters.

Linda is someone who might have benefitted greatly from Photo Voice, both before and after Hurricane Harvey made landfall. As a non-native English speaker, Linda relied heavily on images to guide her understanding of Hurricane Harvey's potential impact as well as when and where to evacuate. English as a Second Language (ESL) speakers like Linda may have a harder time translating their thoughts about their community into English, which in turn would make some of the community resilience assessments previously described (e.g., SWOT analysis, capacity and vulnerability assessments) difficult to participate in unless conducted with other ESL speakers. However, Photo Voice would be a more inclusive assessment for linguistically isolated populations because residents could communicate their thoughts about a community visually rather than verbally.

In addition to its role in helping individuals develop perspective and insight, Photo Voice can be implemented using groups of people who meet weekly to learn how to use a camera and share their photographs. Thus, Photo Voice could enhance participants' self-confidence and embed them in a social network of encouraging and supportive teammates. In Linda's case, her own version of Photo Voice appeared to serve as an outlet to reduce feelings of isolation that were certainly part of her disaster narrative. Remember the photos that Linda shared of her son's muddied bicycle and rain-soaked belongings? We certainly got the sense that Linda *needed* to show us these images. Linda needed someone to see the level of frustration and distress through her eyes. Photo Voice can be therapeutic in the sense that it helps people process their feelings of potentially traumatic events. Given that more than a quarter of the people we talked with reported probable PTSD after Hurricane Harvey, establishing formalized Photo Voice sessions as an alternative to traditional dyadic counseling could yield valuable community feedback on how local government can be more responsive to its citizens. Additionally, Photo Voice may also help local residents process both the trauma in their lives as well as what it takes for them to move forward through both individual and community recovery.

In addition to soliciting feedback from the public in order to inform disaster education and planning, local governments should make concerted structural changes to increase the diversity of the community coalitions used to prepare for, respond to, and recover from disasters. Diverse disaster coalitions are not only important for addressing the multifaceted capacities of resilience, but also for building trust as well as bridging and linking social capital. The economic, social, communication, environmental, and political elements of resilience mean that interdisciplinary or convergent research teams are most likely needed in order to solve the problem of more frequent disasters and aid in the building of community resilience. More importantly, these teams must move beyond their areas of scholarly and professional expertise to consider the lived experiences of the residents they serve.[16]

As an example to consider, recruitment efforts could be designed in such a way that disaster volunteer organizations comprised of lay citizens reflect a variety of identity markers such as race, ethnicity, class, ability, gender, sexual orientation, and nationality. Citizen involvement in community emergency planning may range from serving on citizen advisory committees to volunteering with auxiliary police or fire teams. While racial and ethnic groups may differ in how they prefer to assist with community disaster management, research suggests citizens are willing to participate in helping their community cope with disasters.[17] Therefore, communities must work to invite citizens to participate and feel included in the problem-solving process.

Ultimately, a healthy dialogue must take place between citizens and local government about how best to respond to the community's needs at all disaster phases. The most immediate benefit of researching citizens' needs is emergency management that can use data to develop official and effective messages to help residents understand risks, prepare for disasters, and cope in the aftermath. In addition, when citizens' feedback is solicited or citizens are involved in risk management programs, participants often report more positive feelings toward recovery efforts,[18] as well as an increased sense of belonging and community engagement.[19] Given that residents reported relatively negative perceptions of their community's disaster management and possessed low levels of linking social capital, involving citizens in disaster management plans may have helped to address several cracks in resilience that existed before Hurricane Harvey.

At the Organizational and Community Levels: Emphasize Preparedness

In addition to local government agencies engaging in a dialogue with residents to form stronger relationships and more effective disaster communication plans, civic volunteer organizations can host a variety of programs and events that augment community disaster management efforts. In addition, these strategies can promote citizen disaster communication at the interpersonal level and reinforce the value of volunteer groups that form along the Texas Gulf Coast. While our respondents may not have belonged to a community organization specifically focused on disasters, local residents can still find creative ways to incorporate disaster planning into their own group efforts.

For instance, nearly a quarter of the people we talked with belonged to a parent-teacher association or school group. At first glance, one might assume that the mission of an education-focused organization has nothing to do with disaster preparedness. After all, parent-teacher organizations often assist with school-wide activities like grandparents' day or school carnivals. However, parent-teacher organizations can take this knowledge and expertise in event planning to create school activities that make preparedness fun and exciting for children and families. For instance, Save the Children has developed "Prep Rallies," which include games and other forms of play that educate children on how to prepare for any type of natural disaster.

Organizational interventions, such as education-sponsored disaster preparedness programs, may transcend to other ecological levels outside of school settings. For instance, research has found that disaster education curriculum that encourages children to bring materials or assignments home to discuss disaster preparedness with their parents, guardians, and siblings can help entire households prepare for the next natural disaster.[20] Thus, it is possible that the conversations parents have with their children through activities like these could also generate some of the citizen disaster communication processes we described earlier.

Similarly, more than 25 percent of the people we talked with volunteered with a youth organization, such as scouting. With the Scout motto of "Be Prepared," troop leaders could offer disaster preparedness training to scouts that would provide them with transferable skills and knowledge they could then pass on to their families.[21] Nearly the same number (25 percent) belonged to a neighborhood or crime watch organization. Neighborhood groups are a perfect mechanism for developing a communication infrastructure where local residents can seek information on evacuation plans, identify which residents need immediate assistance, and confirm truthful information and facts about disasters. Many neighborhood groups already have this infrastructure in place. In fact, several people we spoke with had turned to a neighborhood social media page to check in on their neighbors who were thought to be missing or displaced. If a centralized communication resource doesn't exist, neighborhood associations could turn to phone apps like Nextdoor—a private social network for specific neighborhoods, free of charge, that can be downloaded via web and smartphone interfaces. This app provides an easy way for residents who are tangentially connected across neighborhoods to communicate specific needs, alerts, information on missing pets, and general information. The use of this app could prove useful not only during natural disasters, but also during other times when getting the word out or seeking critical information from neighbors is necessary.

Given the high degree of religiosity and church membership along the coast, places of worship could harness their presence in communities to better prepare local residents. We heard a lot about the faith community and the role they played not only in Texas with Hurricane Harvey, but also in places across the country facing other disasters of water, fire, and wind. Faith-based groups are dedicated to serving others, particularly those who are less fortunate. This commitment to service often manifests itself through collecting and distributing canned foods in the fall, toys during the holiday season, and winter clothing during the cold months. In a disaster context, places of worship could ask congregants for donations of items that are useful during an emergency (e.g., flashlights, batteries, first-aid kits, nonperishable food) and assemble home disaster kits to be distributed to lower-income communities. This is just one example of how the daily mission of a faith-based group could align with the goal of increasing household disaster preparedness.

In addition to the faith-based groups, neighborhood associations, and PTAs, several other citizen-focused volunteer groups emerge during disasters—including Katie's "Group to Bring the Marlins Home" in Port Aransas. Emergent volunteer groups can play an important role in assisting existing disaster relief organizations like the Red Cross with building community resilience, but interventions are needed to ensure volunteer groups meet the specific needs of a community's disaster recovery plan. That is, volunteer efforts may be redundant or may be excluded from formal emergency management efforts if their organization does not conform to established organizations' "internal information sharing and accountability structures."[22]

Additionally, emergent volunteer groups may struggle to maintain social ties after volunteers have finished assisting disaster survivors in the post-event phase.[23] Social media platforms can assist in managing and maintaining these emergent citizen volunteer groups. For example, formal disaster relief organizations could use online platforms to share information on the best ways that volunteer groups can help with the recovery process. Moreover, once volunteer efforts dissipate months after a disaster, emergent volunteer groups should maintain their online presence. Continued use of a social media site, such as a Facebook group, allows volunteers to quickly reactivate and organize in case another disaster strikes in the same community or in a nearby location.[24]

At the Organizational and Community Levels: Introduce and Adapt Time Banks

Another way that communities can develop strategies and specific interventions aimed at targeting and bolstering resilience is the implementation of time banking or community currency systems. These systems are often useful in building trust in communities of color, reducing the preparedness gap between those above and below the federal poverty line, and establishing translocal ties before disasters strike. Time banking is a system that does not rely on paying for services through traditional money exchanges. Instead, time bank members pay for services by giving their own time and offering services to others. For example, a person who is registered with a time bank may log hours helping a senior citizen in their community. In exchange for the time spent assisting the senior citizen, that person may "spend" their logged hours receiving assistance from someone else in the community.[25] In general, time banks are one community intervention that can be used to help foster bridging social capital[26] by connecting isolated and low-income individuals in a system where they can offer their talent to a community, meet other time bank members, and receive services they typically would not be able to afford.

Time banks do not have to be disaster-focused, however. We propose that time banks consider addressing specific needs or threats to resilience like those we found across the disaster-affected communities on the Texas Gulf Coast. First, in disaster settings, time banks may be well served to offer services across communities. Such a strategy might prevent high concentrations of resources in more financially secure areas and help establish translocal ties. For example, the neighborhood "stores" that were established in subdivisions like Nottingham Forest helped neighbors who were unquestionably impacted by the hurricane but who were also more likely to hold higher incomes than survivors living in other neighborhoods. As a result, the stores were an example of what Aldrich and Meyer call the dark side of bonding social capital, wherein social cohesion might come at the expense of providing necessary support in other areas of the community.[27] Moreover, the pop-up stores that were created also exemplify what Norris and colleagues highlight as the rule of relative advantage, where the distribution of post-disaster resources is more likely to go to those persons and communities that are already socially, economically, and politically well-connected.[28]

Time banks or other community currency programs can also help incentivize more financially secure residents to distribute their donations of post-disaster supplies to communities that are in more relative need. For instance, what if the Nottingham Forest residents had donated a portion of the supplies in their neighborhood stores to the Houston Area Urban League—where Stacey volunteered to help the low-income residents of Kashmere Gardens? The Nottingham Forest residents could have earned community currency plus a bonus amount because the efforts were going to an area outside of their proximal social network. This type of exchange would have benefitted both communities, while at the same time ensuring that resources or services were distributed to have the maximum impact following a disaster. These systems could specifically focus on eliminating the economic patchworks of preparedness. Clearly, households below the federal poverty line were frequently less prepared, and consequently more vulnerable, to future disasters when compared with other households above the federal poverty line. Data supports this assumption when we looked at who reported increased preparedness since Hurricane Harvey in the Kaiser Family Foundation anniversary survey. If residents who would normally be unable to afford a home disaster kit could exchange community currency for the supplies to assemble such a kit, a significant number of people would be assisted in disaster preparation with little or no cost to the community.

By restructuring time banks and community currency systems to foster the exchange of services across different neighborhoods or communities within a region, this type of community-level intervention may establish translocal ties, or forms of social capital that exist outside of one's neighborhood or community.[29] Inequality in disaster recovery is due, in some part, to differing amounts of translocal social capital between low- and high-income households. Residents with higher incomes are more likely to have transportation and financial resources to travel to other locations outside of the disaster area where family and friends can provide the displaced with material and emotional support. In contrast, households with lower incomes rely heavily on local support. Prolonged recovery can eventually strain local support and deplete resources, so translocal ties become particularly important over time—which, in turn, widens the gap in recovery between those who have the means to travel outside the community compared to those residents who do not.[30]

In order to reduce this significant social resource gap, time banks and community currency systems could serve as a mechanism to help people make connections outside of their immediate neighborhood or city. Time banks and community currency systems have already proven that the programs yield several benefits. In many cases, local systems can aid in introducing people to other residents of different backgrounds,[31] widen one's circle of friends,[32] and increase instrumental social support.[33] If time banks can offer transportation to shuttle people to towns within the same geographic region (e.g., southeastern Texas), it may be possible to replicate those benefits translocally. In fact, people who transport other residents to different towns for other time bank projects could apply their personal transportation as a service that would qualify for deposits into their local time bank or community currency system.

At the time this chapter was written, time banks and community currency systems are nearly nonexistent in Texas. The sole Texas time bank chapter exists in Denton, which is four and a half hours away from Houston and recorded its last exchange of services a few weeks before the arrival of Hurricane Harvey. At one point, Houston also had a community currency system called Houston Hours, but the program became inactive.[34] The paucity of time bank and community currency systems along the Texas Gulf Coast presents opportunities and challenges, but these programs could be extremely important to the future response and recovery of communities all along the coast. The absence of such programs means communities do not have to adapt current systems; instead, they can create time bank programs specifically targeted to address the social and economic divisions that emerged during disaster recovery. Nevertheless, the absence of time banks in the Texas Gulf Coast means it will take some time to set them up, develop a system to manage the hours and services residents provide, and attract participants to ensure the development of a robust program.

At the National Level: Recovery Loss or Mitigation?

National disaster interventions currently emphasize funding communities after disasters strike. However, citizens and the communities where they reside may be better served if the federal government were to invest more in mitigating disaster consequences rather than figuring out strategies to assist in recovering losses.[35] Past research, as well as our own findings, illustrates the need to focus on mitigation. As previously mentioned, federally subsidized flood insurance and disaster relief programs create little incentive for local governments to invest in mitigation efforts.[36] This is not surprising particularly when nearly a third of US residents report an unwillingness to contribute any money to improve local preparedness. This reluctance is, in part, because residents perceive that their taxes are already too high, an additional cost would be untenable, and the government is a poor steward of taxpayer dollars.[37] Actually, citizens often create an incentive for elected officials to opt for funding recovery over mitigation because voters tend to favor an incumbent presidential party that secures disaster aid for communities.[38] Thus, we tend to focus more on what someone did after the storm than what they didn't do before the storm.

Based on the unfavorable reviews of the federal government in both the Kaiser Family Foundation data and our interviews, we can extrapolate that as a society we expect the federal government to spend and act immediately following a disaster. The federal government has a role to play in disaster management even as FEMA endorses the Whole Community approach. Moreover, it is not a false choice between providing disaster relief and funding mitigation efforts. The federal government has to do both. Rather, government should work to provide more of that funding before disasters strike.

Time for Action

Something must change. Somehow, we need to do a better job when it comes to learning from our mistakes. We can't keep letting communities and their residents struggle to prepare themselves for disasters. We need to develop and implement resilience and preparedness plans that are tailored to specific needs, people, and places. This will require some creative thinking and the willingness on the part of all actors to engage in a dialogue of solution rather than finger-pointing. It may mean sending individuals or teams of individuals into communities to talk with community members, learn from them, and find out what they need and don't need. Once this process of discovery is complete, then government agencies and organizational partners can work together to develop an approach that is tailored to individual communities—one that will be responsive to their specific needs rather than some shotgun, one-size-fits-all approach.

Throughout this book, we have listened to survivors tell their stories. Most of them have benefitted greatly from their neighbors. Some of those neighbors they actually knew, but in many cases, they did not know them until they found themselves in the middle of the terror and destruction heading their way. Others benefitted from the help of total strangers, nonprofits, churches, businesses, and local recovery groups that showed up, rolled up their sleeves, and asked what they could do to help. For some survivors, social capital was abundant. All the data from our work and the work of the Kaiser Family Foundation suggests that bonding social capital was more available than bridging or linking social capital. Those who had fewer resources before the storm made landfall tended to report experiences and tell stories that suggested their social capital and social ties were strained, deteriorated, and limited, with a finite amount of resources available to them both during and after the hurricane.

Another important part of the recovery story that we heard from survivors had to do with questions about what the state and federal governments did to plan, prepare, and execute both during and after Hurricane Harvey. Comments like these from two anonymous respondents were typical of residents when asked about government response:

I honestly believe my community was not prepared for such an event. My community tried to do what they could, but even with a hurricane like Harvey it would have took much more planning, and much more resources. I still don't know what the state government's response was. My community is small. You see the response by these governments in the larger metropolitan areas but in the little communities, I didn't really see any response. I'm not saying they didn't respond; I'm just saying I didn't see a direct response to the disaster in our community.

The government did okay. FEMA helped us a bit, but I felt like this process of assistance was not very consistent. I know a lot of families in my neighborhood who had their homes flooded, and received very little help from FEMA. While other families didn't really have extensive damage yet received more than $30,000 in FEMA assistance. It just seemed like there wasn't any rhyme or reason with respect to who got what and why.

It bears repeating that we need to do something—the status quo is just not good enough, and it may in fact unfairly favor certain groups or locations over others.[39] The development of a resilient community and its response to natural disasters should not be determined by degrees of segregation or inequality but rather by fairness, equality, and need. So this leaves us with many questions and not many answers. It leaves us scratching our heads and wondering when things are going to change and who the force behind those changes will be.

Our intention for this book is to catalyze. Like so many others, we want to see real, effective, directed change. We have spelled out some potential interventions that can be offered up across an ecological landscape that include individuals and governments, as well as organizations and citizen groups. But where will that take us?

We hope a few takeaways will remain at the forefront of any conversation addressing natural disaster resilience, response, and recovery. We have some insights from our brief examination of this disaster based on what people told us about their experiences. The respondents we were fortunate to meet and whose words we were fortunate to read serve as reminders as well as suggestions of how to move forward toward stronger, more effective processes of preparation, recovery, and rebuilding.

Race, Place, and Disasters

Katrina was different. Ike was different. Hazel was different. Sandy was different. Hugo was different. Major destructive hurricanes like these remind us that natural disasters are not all things to all people or places. The destruction that took place in the Ninth Ward in New Orleans during Hurricane Katrina was different from what happened along the New Jersey shoreline when Hurricane Sandy made landfall. During Harvey, what happened on the outskirts of Corpus Christi was different from what happened in downtown Houston. What happened to those living in North Houston was different from what happened to the neighborhoods and the residents of southeastern Houston. No matter how we tell the tale, *place matters*. It matters because of the physical positioning of some communities compared to others. It matters because of the housing stock and infrastructure in some communities compared to others. It matters because, in some neighborhoods, a lot of money is at stake and at work so that cleanup and rebuilding appear to progress at warp speed compared to other neighborhoods. It also matters because of the degree of segregation, inequality, and social structural forces at work that continue to create unequal and unfair distribution of resources across communities, that have some benefitting from resilience planning and others left with little or no plans to use in preparation for the next inevitable disaster.

What can we do to change the storyline? How can we help the most physically and economically challenged neighborhoods meet the demands and face the complexities of cleanup and rebuilding? Is it just about money? How important is social capital to rebuilding and recovery in the history of hurricanes in the United States? Are we preparing the next generation for what is likely to be a much worse period of time in terms of natural disasters, particularly as climate change impacts populations living in or around major metropolitan areas and coastal regions of the United States? We must ask these critical questions now—not after the next natural disaster, or the next, or the next.

We listened to survivors tell many different stories. While tragedy, loss, and destruction were consistent themes, we also heard about the different places where people experienced the storm. We heard from people living in apartment complexes that lacked flood control, as well as people living in suburban neighborhoods that banded together and watched over one another's property. Some neighborhoods lay in ruin six months after the storm, while other neighborhoods began rebuilding right away and already look as though they have been restored. Segregation, income inequality, old housing stock, crumbling infrastructure, and little or no community/residential planning vision represented a perfect storm of social and physical circumstances that impacted neighborhoods and communities up and down the Texas coast. Places that escaped the watchful eye of City Hall, regional planning commissions, or public works were the places struggling to recover after the storm and are still struggling to recover nearly two years later.

With the two-year anniversary of Harvey already passed, we are still hearing from residents about their experiences. Many are still suffering through the bureaucratic quagmire to get their homes, communities, schools, businesses, roadways, and more rebuilt. Some feel abandoned, while others feel blessed. One anonymous resident summed it up like this:

> I feel blessed to have the neighbors I have who helped us recover, rebuild, and revive. But not everyone was as lucky as we were. I know people who are getting ripped off by contractors and other shady businesses just looking to make a buck. The stories we heard were depressing. Even the government seemed to be doing more for some and less for others. I guess it depends on who you are but that is no different than anywhere you go or anything you do. I know of one guy that was offered $400 in assistance after literally losing everything. Another homeowner who needed just minor repairs was able to save 60 percent of their belongings in a two-story home and they were given nearly $3,000 in assistance. Try and figure that one out!

The Kaiser Family Foundation and the Episcopal Health Foundation went back to the Texas Gulf Coast and talked to survivors as a follow-up to their earlier survey in October 2017.[40] At the one-year anniversary mark, their survey shed light on the longer-term recovery needs of those residents who were still struggling to put their homes and lives back together. Even the more recent Kaiser survey found significant differences in the road to recovery based on where people were living at the time or where they were rebuilding. For example, the Kaiser survey found that many residents living in the Golden Triangle (Orange, Jefferson, and Hardin Counties) east of Houston where the cities of Beaumont, Orange, and Port Arthur are located were still struggling, and more than three in ten residents reported that their lives were still disrupted by the aftermath of Hurricane Harvey nearly a year later. No one wants to see headlines suggesting that some communities are getting more recovery assistance and more federal dollars compared to others. These headlines are even more problematic when the implication is that larger, minority, poorer communities are the ones who have received the short end of the recovery stick. In their October 2018 report, CityLab acknowledges that their sample was small and non-representative of Texas Gulf Coast cities impacted by the storm; however, their findings are troubling and indicative of the consistent theme that has emerged in this book regarding the intersection of race and place.

One Size Does Not Fit All

Yes, structured inequality plays a role in the preparedness, response, and recovery processes across communities—yet no single solution or strategy for preparing, recovering, and rebuilding communities impacted by a natural disaster exists. Effective strategies can be partly determined by the resources that communities have available to them, the social capital and social resource capacity of the residents to stay and rebuild, and the capacity of cities and towns to support the rebuilding of not only homes and businesses but also the core infrastructure. Do the streets and sidewalks need to be replaced or just cleaned? Does the storm sewer system need to be replaced and expanded or just updated? Recovery and rebuilding is a complicated process that needs to be tailored to the specific needs of neighborhoods with the development of a comprehensive plan to build and maintain resilient communities.

Government officials and emergency managers must engage community members in discussions about risk and disaster planning. Every community would do well to start by asking its residents what they need in order to be better informed, better prepared, and more self-reliant in the face of a natural disaster. Nearly half of our respondents did not believe their community tried to prevent or prepare for future disasters.

Even if municipal governments had emergency plans in place, this finding suggests the average citizen was not invited to, involved with, or invested in a community's disaster management planning. In such moments, the average citizen slips through the cracks of even the most well-intentioned efforts to protect a community during a disaster. Emergency management approaches must make herculean efforts to tailor their plans to fit the community's unique needs. If communities like Port Arthur had included residents in disaster planning conversations, they might have been able to better predict the types of obstacles that would prevent evacuees from returning to their community.

Learning from Our Mistakes

Can we *please* stop making the same mistakes every time a hurricane strikes? Our country has volumes of pages in its history books from which to learn. The US has experienced massive natural disasters that have marked the unfortunate destruction and redevelopment of cities all along our coastlines. Nevertheless, it appears we are repeating our mistakes and learning little along the way. We see this debate unfolding in Houston right now as the city balances two needs: (1) to mitigate future hurricane damage, and (2) to manage the burgeoning housing needs of a growing population. In April 2018, the Houston City Council passed new floodplain regulations as an initial strategy to balance the needs of hurricane preparedness in the context of a booming urban population. But the plan appeared to appease no one. While the new regulation would require developers to build homes at an elevated level, two feet above the five-hundred-year storm level to be precise, the council's decision would also allow the city to build yet again on a floodplain that will certainly be susceptible to the torrential downpour of future hurricanes.[41]

Simultaneously, in an effort to correct for a lack of disaster planning, the well-intentioned yet stricter standards put some residents at risk of making the difficult decision between rebuilding and relocating. While it is positive that people feel attached to the homes where they raised families and want to stay in neighborhoods where their neighbors have become friends, many residents may not be able to afford the costly improvements that go along with raising the levels of their homes just to be able to stay in a floodplain. In turn, households with higher incomes will certainly have the advantage and opportunity to stay, while those experiencing significant and complicated needs with limited incomes will be forced to migrate and remain permanently displaced from their Texas Gulf Coast homes.

So Where Do We Go from Here?

What if the next time a disaster loomed we engaged in a different type of evacuation plan? What if we purposely addressed the needs of those residents who, because they lack access to personal transportation or an ability to locate friends and relatives to stay with, are just unable to help themselves? We know a significant part of the population typically gets left behind or needs to be rescued. Even worse, some will perish in more storms like Harvey. These residents are often part of the poorer, disenfranchised, minority populations living in large urban centers.

While empirical data would certainly bear this out, the majority of people who perished in natural disasters like Hurricane Harvey, Irma, Maria, Florence, and Michael were the ones who could not leave. They had to tie down their mobile homes, climb in the closets of their apartment, or hunker down in shelters and pray for the storm to miss them. Hurricanes Katrina and Harvey have left indelible marks—marks of inadequacy, unpreparedness, and inequality. Rich, white people are typically not the victims of natural disaster, and while that is a difficult pill to swallow, it is probably as truthful a perspective as any being offered regarding disaster displacement and recovery. While this book has been a story about race, it has also told a story about wealth and the way money continues to influence our decision-making, both prior to and long after the tragedy of storms like Hurricane Harvey.

So instead of relying on standard methods of warning that are inaccessible to some citizens, perhaps local governments should engage public transportation, private transportation (Uber, Lyft, etc.), and the National Guard in a coordinated evacuation plan. Or maybe instead of assuming citizens can take care of themselves or find someone else to help them, the city could provide direct support that specifically targets the places that are at the greatest risk for flooding and destruction. Instead of assuming people will tell one another about flood insurance or that neighborhoods and communities will develop comprehensive plans to evacuate, why not provide them with a concrete exit strategy?

What about developing strategies to house evacuees in places other than temporary warehouses? Why not transport them to large hotels that are willing to work closely with FEMA and implement comprehensive relocation centers that can temporarily provide shelter and services for persons who have been displaced? What if evacuees were assigned to specific teams that helped to coordinate displacement and relocation, remaining part of that team until everyone was relocated or returned home? Not every disaster has to end the same way. Careful planning, community engagement, an active and readied government, and disaster preparation agencies are all part of an equation that needs to be balanced regardless of place, circumstance, or population composition.

Which Leaves Us All Where?

Acknowledging the risks related to where people live, endorsing place-based initiatives that develop strategies to assist those who often cannot help themselves, and helping to garner resources and social capital necessary to change a community's disaster recovery trajectory should be at the core of any program designed to make a difference in the disaster relief and recovery of a community and its residents. At the core of what we have consistently heard throughout the stories, narratives, and survivor responses was that formal relief infrastructure is important but unevenly distributed.

Communities do not automatically operate from the same starting point, receiving the same resources, with the expectation of a quick recovery that returns everyone and everything back to "normal." However, the recovery and resilience strategies we discussed earlier that are about what individuals can and can't do in making a difference are critical. They are replicable and can be developed regardless of where one lives. These individually driven systems are about doing the best one can—so residents take charge, support one another, and help one another during the process of preparation and recovery. While disaster relief is often about waiting for FEMA, the Red Cross, or some other disaster relief agency to step in and help, some of the most successful and moving stories we heard were simply about people making recovery happen the best they could, with whatever they had, and with whomever they knew.

Where does this leave us? We must stop waiting for something to happen. We have to stop assuming that FEMA, the state/local government, emergency management, or some other organization will always have our backs. We have to start mobilizing differently than we have in the past. We have to start taking charge of our own readiness, the community's readiness, and find ways to empower and connect with neighbors who can do a lot more for each other when they are connected in advance than when they have to scramble. Waiting for the next disaster to happen and then changing the way we do things after the fact is no different from assuming things will get better on their own. They won't.

In the face of the devastation of the 2017 US hurricane season and the growing reports out of Puerto Rico, some may argue that the Harvey response and recovery was a paragon of disaster management. Our data and stories, however, do not suggest that. Rather, Hurricane Harvey served as a grim reminder of what can happen when we don't change our strategies for preparedness, or we don't change our strategies to ensure an equitable recovery, or we don't change the old way of thinking about relief and recovery. We clearly need to find a new, more innovative, citizen-driven approach that embraces connectedness and resilience. Together we must forge a new pathway to preparedness, relief, and recovery.

ACKNOWLEDGMENTS

This research was funded by the National Science Foundation NSF1760185; RAPID: *Capital, Coping, and the Displaced: Health, Well-Being, and Resiliency Among Hurricane Harvey Evacuees*. We appreciate the support of the National Science Foundation in recognizing the importance of funding this work in a timely manner. In addition, we acknowledge the support, assistance, and insight of several individuals and organizations that have been supportive and helpful to the development and completion of this project. We would like to thank the University of Arkansas, the J. William Fulbright College of Arts and Sciences, the Department of Sociology and Criminology, and the Department of Communication for creating the type of intellectual environment necessary to do the work contained within these pages.

We would also like to single out and thank several individuals, including Michael Drager, project coordinator, who was extraordinarily valuable in directing the early phases of our field work, coordinating interviewers, securing interviews, navigating the Texas Gulf Coast traffic, and staying on with us until the job was done. We would like to thank the interviewers who worked tirelessly to secure as many face-to-face interviews as they could in a relatively short time frame and amid the chaos of recovery. In addition, we would like to thank the countless organizations, service providers, local governments, and individuals who gave of their time and energy to help us tell this story. Without that support while we were on the coast, this project would not have been completed. We appreciate the early support on this project from our colleague, Xuan Shi, whose patience and expertise helped advance our data collection and forward-thinking about a place-sensitive individual survivor data collection. A big thank you to our outside copy editor, Jocelyn Bailey, who spent hours shaping and reshaping this roughed-out story to a sharpened, focused work. She helped us pay attention to detail, while giving us one more grammar lesson that would forever make up for what we missed in our primary and secondary educations. We also want to express our deep-felt thanks to our graduate students, Diana Cascante, Aiden Lister, Jill Neiemier, Jessica Paschal, and Reilly Gibson for doing all that we asked them to do and then some. The countless hours that this team logged preparing, analyzing, and organizing data and tables, making sure that all the references looked the same and were meticulously prepared and cross-checked, and then did all the background work necessary for the manuscript, is greatly appreciated.

We would especially like to thank the publication team at NYU Press. Their dedication to developing and delivering quality work is what attracted us to them in the first place, and we are extremely grateful for their careful handling of this project. In particular, thanks to our executive editor, Illene Kalish. Her commitment to our ideas and dedication to delivering the final product in a timely manner is appreciated.

Finally, we want to thank our families for their tireless support and commitment to our pursuit of knowledge and the telling of this important story.

NOTES

PREFACE
1 Cutter et al. 2008; Donner and Lavariega-Montforti 2018; Finch et al. 2010; Van Zandt et al. 2012.
2 Fitzpatrick and LaGory 2011; Kawachi et al. 2008; Putnam 2000; Putnam and Feldstein 2003.

CHAPTER 1. A HARD RAIN'S A-GONNA FALL
1 Governor's Commission to Rebuild Texas 2018.
2 Samenow 2017.
3 Maas 2017.
4 Fitzpatrick and LaGory 2011; Jokinen-Gordon 2013; Kawachi and Berkman 2003; Sampson 2012.
5 Fitzpatrick and LaGory 2011; Kawachi et al. 2008; Putnam 2000; Putnam and Feldstein 2003.
6 Finch et al. 2010; Jones-DeWeever and Hartmann 2006; Tierney 2014.
7 Fitzpatrick and LaGory 2011.
8 Chakraborty et al. 2019a; Cutter et al. 2008; Donner and Lavariega-Montforti 2018; Finch et al. 2010; Van Zandt et al. 2012.
9 Chakraborty et al. 2019b; Collins et al. 2018; Elliott and Pais 2006.
10 For a discussion of the intersection of race, class, and gender and how social vulnerability shaped Katrina disaster response and recovery, see Finch et al. 2010.
11 Chakraborty et al. 2019a.
12 Ross and Clay 2018.
13 National Academies of Sciences, Engineering, and Medicine 2019.
14 Aldrich 2012; Erickson 1976; McFarlane and Norris 2006; Turner 1976.
15 Juan 2018.
16 Aldrich 2012; Finch et al. 2010; Peacock and Girard 2000.
17 NCEI 2019.
18 Barclay 2017.
19 Holthaus 2017.
20 Mann et al. 2017.
21 Elliot and Pais 2006; Finch et al. 2010; Peacock et al. 1997.
22 Fitzpatrick and LaGory 2011; Massey and Denton 1993; Molotch et al. 2000; Sampson 2012.

23 Brinkley 2006; Dyson 2005; Horne 2006; Rivlin 2015.
24 Spialek and Houston 2018.

CHAPTER 2. WHO WE ARE

1 Donner and Diaz 2018; Padgett 2002; Richardson et al. 2012; Rosaria 2018.
2 Lardieri 2017.
3 Aldrich 2012.
4 Lozano 2018.
5 Chakaborty et al. 2019b.

CHAPTER 3. EVERY PICTURE TELLS A STORY

1 Linda, phone conversation, March 1, 2018.
2 Burch 2018.
3 Anonymous, House of Hope resident, 2018.
4 Chamlee-Wright and Storr 2009; Norris et al. 2008.
5 Juan 2018.
6 Kaiser Family Foundation 2017.
7 Kaiser Family Foundation 2017.
8 Anonymous Houston homeowner, October 23, 2017.
9 Marta, rural Texas resident, May 5, 2018.
10 DeWolfe 2000.
11 Patricia, Houston resident, May 5, 2018.
12 Anonymous Port Arthur resident, April 2018.
13 Rayelynn, Bayside resident, May 5, 2018.
14 Kaiser Family Foundation 2017.
15 Fifty-nine-year-old black female, Beaumont resident.

CHAPTER 4. ANTICIPATION

1 FEMA 2011.
2 Norris et al. 2008; Pfefferbaum et al. 2015.
3 Norris et al. 2008.
4 Putnam 1995:664–65.
5 Kim and Kang 2010; Spittal et al. 2008.
6 Kasperson et al. 1988.
7 Brenkert-Smith et al. 2013.
8 Houston et al. 2015b.
9 Kaiser Family Foundation 2017.
10 Aldrich and Meyer 2015.
11 Passel and Cohn 2017.
12 Theodore 2017.
13 Norris et al. 2008.
14 Houston et al. 2015b; Nicholls 2012.
15 Houston 2012.

16 Spialek and Houston 2018.
17 Aldrich 2012; Szreter and Woolcock 2004.
18 Olsen 2018.
19 Atkiss et al. 2019.
20 FEMA 2014.
21 FEMA 2015.
22 Bagstad et al. 2007.
23 National Research Council 2014.
24 Blessing et al. 2017.
25 Bagstad et al. 2007.
26 Burby 2006.
27 Boburg and Reinhard 2017.
28 Blessing et al. 2017; National Research Council 2014.

CHAPTER 5. WHO'LL STOP THE RAIN?
1 DHS 2018.
2 Fullilove and Saul 2006.
3 Fullilove and Saul 2006:168.
4 Mouw 2006.
5 Hawkins and Maurer 2010.
6 Aldrich and Meyer 2015.
7 Gurwitch et al. 2007:27.
8 Spence et al. 2007.
9 Hilfinger Messias et al. 2012.
10 Elliott et al. 2010.
11 Elliott et al. 2010.
12 Hawkins and Maurer 2010.
13 Elliott et al. 2010.
14 Kaiser Family Foundation 2017.
15 Manyena et al. 2011; Norris et al. 2008.

CHAPTER 6. AFTER THE STORM
1 Liu 2009.
2 Houston et al. 2012.
3 Swartz 2018.
4 Manyena et al. 2011.
5 APA 2013.
6 Neria et al. 2008.
7 Bonanno et al. 2010.
8 Elliot and Pais 2006.
9 Chakraborty et al. 2019a.
10 CEHI 2019.
11 Weiss 2007.

12 Schwartz et al. 2018.
13 Capps 2018.
14 Capps 2018.
15 Boscarino et al. 2004.
16 Houston et al. 2015a; Rosellini et al. 2014.
17 CEHI 2019.
18 CEHI 2019.
19 CEHI 2019.
20 Tedeschi and Calhoun 2004:1.
21 First et al. 2018.
22 Tedeschi and Calhoun 1996.
23 Joyce 2018.
24 Hersher 2018.
25 Kim and Kang 2010.
26 Bourque et al. 2013.
27 Witte 1992.
28 Mulilis and Duval 1997.
29 Spence et al. 2011.
30 Kaiser Family Foundation 2018.

CHAPTER 7. CHANGES

1 Livingston 2019.
2 Willis 2019.
3 FEMA 2011.
4 NCEI 2018.
5 Houston et al. 2015b.
6 Sallis et al. 2008.
7 Sallis et al. 2008:482.
8 Spialek and Houston 2018.
9 Spialek and Houston 2019; Houston et al. 2017.
10 Spialek et al. 2019.
11 Littlefield et al. 2010.
12 Kuehnert 2018.
13 Kuehnert 2018.
14 Pfefferbaum et al. 2011.
15 Wang and Burris 1997.
16 DeSimone and Farrell 2014.
17 Perry and Mushkatel 1986.
18 Kweit and Kweit 2004.
19 Liu et al. 2017.
20 Ronan and Johnston 2003; Ronan et al. 2010.
21 Jang et al. 2012.
22 Schmidt et al. 2018:345.

23 Lai 2019.
24 Lai 2019.
25 Collom 2005; Lasker et al. 2011.
26 Aldrich and Meyer 2015.
27 Aldrich and Meyer 2015.
28 Norris et al. 2008.
29 Elliott et al. 2010.
30 Elliott et al. 2010.
31 Collom 2008.
32 Jacob et al. 2004.
33 Collom et al. 2012.
34 Collom 2005.
35 Miao 2018.
36 Burby 2006.
37 Donahue 2014.
38 Healy and Malhotra 2009.
39 Chakraborty et al. 2019a; Finch et al. 2010; Horowitz 2017.
40 Kaiser Family Foundation 2018.
41 Wilson 2018.

REFERENCES

Acosta, Jim, and Sophie Tatum. 2017. "Source: Trump's Puerto Rico Tweets Were Response to San Juan Mayor." *CNN*, October 13. www.cnn.com.
Aldrich, Daniel P. 2012. *Building Resilience: Social Capital in Post-Disaster Recovery*. Chicago: University of Chicago Press.
Aldrich, Daniel P., and Michelle A. Meyer. 2015. "Social Capital and Community Resilience. *American Behavioral Scientist* 59:254–69. DOI:10.1177/0002764214550299.
APA (American Psychiatric Association). 2013. *Diagnostic and Statistical Manual of Mental Disorders*. 5th ed. Washington, DC: APA.
Atkiss, Katy, Kate Vickery, and Jeff Stys. 2019. *Humanitarian Action Plan: A Coordinated Disaster Response Plan to Serve Immigrants of the Greater Houston Region*. Houston, TX: Houston Immigration Legal Services Collaborative. https://hap.houstonimmigration.org.
Bagstad, Kenneth J., Kevin Stapleton, and John R. D'Agostino. 2007. "Taxes, Subsidies, and Insurance as Drivers of United States Coastal Development." *Ecological Economics* 63(2):285–98. DOI:10.1016/j.ecolecon.2006.09.019.
Barclay, Eliza. 2017. "Harvey Is Part of a Pattern of Extreme Weather Scientists Saw Coming. They're Still Shocked." *Vox*, August 31. www.vox.com.
Blessing, Russell, Antonia Sebastian, and Samuel Brody. 2017. "Flood Risk Delineation in the United States: How Much Loss Are We Capturing?" *Natural Hazards Review* 18(3):04017002. DOI:10.1061/(ASCE)NH.1527-6996.0000242.
Boburg, Shawn, and Beth Reinhard. 2017. "Houston's 'Wild West' Growth: How the City's Development May have Contributed to Devastating Flooding." *Washington Post*. www.washingtonpost.com.
Bonanno, George A., Chris Brewin, Krzysztof Kaniasty, and Annette M. La Greca. 2010. "Weighing the Costs of Disaster: Consequences, Risks, and Resilience in Individuals, Families, and Communities." *Psychological Sciences in the Public Interest* 11:1–49. DOI:10.1177/1529100610387086.
Boscarino, Joseph A., Charles R. Figley, and Richard E. Adams. 2004. "Compassion Fatigue Following the September 11 Terrorist Attacks: A Study of Secondary Trauma among New York City Social Workers." *International Journal of Emergency Mental Health* 6:57–66.
Bourque, Linda B., Rotrease Regan, Melissa M. Kelley, Michele M. Wood, Megumi Kano, and Dennis S. Mileti. 2013. "An Examination of the Effect of Perceived Risk on Preparedness Behavior." *Environment and Behavior* 45:615–49. DOI:10.1177/0013916512437596.

Brenkert-Smith, Hannah, Katherine L. Dickinson, Patricia A. Champ, and Nicholas Flores. 2013. "Social Amplification of Wildfire Risk: The Role of Social Interactions and Information Sources." *Risk Analysis* 33:800–817. DOI:10.1111/j.1539-6924.2012.01917.

Brinkley, Douglas. 2006. *The Great Deluge: Hurricane Katrina, New Orleans, and Mississippi Gulf Coast*. New York: Harper Perennial.

Brulliard, Karin. 2017. "Harvey Is Also Displacing Snakes, Fire Ants and Gators." *Washington Post*, August 28. www.washingtonpost.com.

Burby, Raymond J. 2006. "Hurricane Katrina and the Paradoxes of Government Disaster Policy: Bringing about Wise Governmental Decisions for Hazardous Areas." *ANNALS of the American Academy of Political and Social Sciences* 604:171–91. DOI:10.1177/0002716205284676.

Burch, Audra. 2018. "Brutal Choice in Houston: Sell Home at a Loss or Face New Floods." *New York Times*, March 30. www.nytimes.com.

Capps, Kriston. 2018. "Why Are These Tiny Towns Getting So Much Hurricane Harvey Aid?" *CityLab*, October 3. www.citylab.com.

CEHI (Children's Environmental Health Initiative). 2019. *Hurricane Harvey Registry Initial Report*. https://harveyregistry.rice.edu/.

Chakraborty, Jayajit, Sara E. Grineski, and Timothy W. Collins. 2019a. "Hurricane Harvey and People with Disabilities: Disproportionate Exposure to Flooding in Houston, Texas." *Social Science and Medicine* 226:176–81. DOI:10.1016/j.socscimed.2019.02.039.

Chakraborty, Jayajit, Timothy W. Collins, and Sara E. Grineski. 2019b. "Exploring the Environmental Justice Implications of Hurricane Harvey Flooding in Greater Houston, Texas." *American Journal of Public Health* 109:244–50. DOI:10.2105/AJPH.2018.304846.

Chamlee-Wright, Emily, and Virgil H. Storr. 2009. "There's No Place like New Orleans: Sense of Place and Community Recovery in the Ninth Ward after Hurricane Katrina." *Journal of Urban Affairs* 31:615–34. DOI:10.1111/j.1467-9906.2009.00479.

Collins, Timothy W., Sara E. Grineski, and Jayajit Chakraborty. 2018. "Environmental Injustice and Flood Risk: A Conceptual Model and Case Comparison of Metropolitan Miami and Houston, USA." *Regulatory Environmental Change* 18:311–23. DOI:10.1007/s10113-017-1121-9.

Collom, Ed. 2005. "Community Currency in the United States: The Social Environment in which It Emerges and Survives." *Environment and Planning A: Economy and Space* 37:1565–87. DOI:10.1068/a37172.

Collom, Ed. 2008. "Engagement of the Elderly in Time Banking: The Potential for Social Capital Generation in an Aging Society." *Journal of Aging and Social Policy* 20:414–36. DOI:10.1080/08959420802186282.

Collom, Ed, Judith N. Lasker, and Corinne Kyriacou. 2012. *Equal Time, Equal Value: Community Currencies and Time Banking in the US*. Farnham, UK: Ashgate.

Cutter, Susan L., Christopher G. Burton, and Christopher T. Emrich. 2010. "Disaster Resilience Indicators for Benchmarking Baseline Conditions." *Journal of Homeland Security and Emergency Management* 7:1–22. DOI: 10.2202/1547-7355.1732.

Cutter, Susan L., Lindsey Barnes, Melissa Berry, Christopher Burton, Elijah Evans, Eric Tate, and Jennifer Webb. 2008. "A Place-Based Model for Understanding Community Resilience to Natural Disasters." *Global Environmental Change* 18(4): 598–606. DOI:10.1016/j.gloenvcha.2008.07.013.

DeSimone, Joseph M., and Crista L. Farrell. 2014. "Driving Convergence with Human Diversity." *Science Translation Medicine* 6:1–2.

DeWolfe, Deborah J. 2000. *Training Manual for Mental Health and Human Service Workers in Major Disasters*. 2nd ed. HHS Publication No. ADM 90-538. Rockville, MD: US Department of Health and Human Services, Substance Abuse and Mental Health Services Administration, Center for Mental Health Services.

DHS (Department of Homeland Security). 2018. *The Whole Community: Individuals with Disabilities in Disaster Response and Recovery*. Washington, DC: US Government. https://www.dhs.gov.

Donahue, Amy K. 2014. "Risky Business: Willingness to Pay for Disaster Preparedness." *Public Budgeting & Finance* 34:100–119. DOI:10.1111/pbaf.12051.

Donner, William R., and Jessica Lavariega-Montforti. 2018. "Ethnicity, Income, and Disaster Preparedness in Deep South Texas, United States." *Disasters* 42:719–33. DOI:10.1111/disa.12277.

Donner, William R., and Walter Diaz. 2018. "Methodological Issues in Disaster Research." Pp. 289–309 in *Handbook of Disaster Research: Handbooks in Sociology and Social Research*, edited by H. Rodriquez, W. Donner, and J. Trainor. New York: Springer.

Dyson, Michael Eric. 2005. *Come Hell or High Water: Hurricane Katrina and the Color of Disaster*. New York: Basic Civitas.

Economist. 2017. "Hurricane Harvey Has Exposed The Inadequacy of Flood Insurance." September 9. www.economist.com.

Elliott, James R., and Jeremy Pais. 2006. "Race, Class, and Hurricane Katrina: Social Differences in Human Responses to Disaster." *Social Science Research* 35(2):295–321. DOI:10.1016/j.ssresearch.2006.02.003.

Elliott, James R., Timothy J. Haney, and Petrice Sams-Abiodun. 2010. "Limits to Social Capital: Comparing Network Assistance in Two New Orleans Neighborhoods Devastated by Hurricane Katrina." *Sociological Quarterly* 51:624–48. DOI:10.1111/j.1533-8525.2010.01186.x.

Erikson, Kai T. 1976. *Everything in Its Path: Destruction of Community in the Buffalo Creek Flood*. New York: Simon & Schuster.

FEMA (Federal Emergency Management Agency). 2011. *A Whole Community Approach to Emergency Management: Principles, Themes, and Pathways for Action*. Washington, DC: US Department of Homeland Security. https://fema.gov.

FEMA (Federal Emergency Management Agency). 2014. *Preparedness in America: Research Insights to Increase Individual, Organizational, and Community Action*. Washington, DC: US Department of Homeland Security. https://fema.gov.

FEMA (Federal Emergency Management Agency). 2015. *Flood Insurance: How It Works*. Washington, DC: US Department of Homeland Security. https://fema.gov.

Finch, Christina, Christopher T. Emrich, and Susan L. Cutter. 2010. "Disaster Disparities and Differential Recovery in New Orleans." *Population Environment* 31:179–202. DOI:10.1007/s11111-009-0099-8.

First, Jennifer, Nathan First, Jordan Stevens, Vicky Mieseler, and J. Brian Houston. 2018. "Post-Traumatic Growth 2.5 Years after the 2011 Joplin, Missouri Tornado." *Journal of Family Social Work* 21:5–21. DOI:10.1080/10522158.2017.1402529.

Fitzpatrick, Kevin M., and Mark LaGory. 2011. *Unhealthy Cities: Poverty, Race, and Place in America*. New York: Routledge.

Foxhall, Emily. 2018. "Coast Still in Harvey's Grip." *Houston Chronicle*, August 25.

Fritz, Angela, and Jason Samenow. 2017. "Harvey Unloaded 33 Trillion Gallons of Water in the U.S." *Washington Post*, September 2. www.washingtonpost.com.

Fullilove, M. T., and J. Saul. 2006. "Rebuilding Communities Post-Disaster in New York." Pp. 164–77 in *9/11: Mental health in Wake of Terrorist Attacks*, edited by Y. Neria, R. Gross, and R. D. Marshall. New York: Cambridge University Press.

Governor's Commission to Rebuild Texas. 2018. *Eye of the Storm: Report of the Governor's Commission to Rebuild Texas*. Texas A&M University System, College Station, TX. www.rebuildtexas.today.

Gurwitch, R. H., B. Pfefferbaum, J. M. Montgomery, R. W. Klomp, and D. B. Reissman. 2007. *Building Community Resilience for Children and Families*. Oklahoma City, OK: Terrorism and Disaster Center, University of Oklahoma Health Sciences Center.

Hawkins, Robert L., and Katherine Maurer. 2010. "Bonding, Bridging, and Linking: How Social Capital Operated in New Orleans following Hurricane Katrina." *British Journal of Social Work* 40:1777–93. DOI:10.1093/bjsw/bcp087.

Healy, Andrew, and Neil Malhotra. 2009. "Myopic Voters and Natural Disaster Policy." *American Political Science Review* 103:387–406. DOI:10.1017/S0003055409990104.

Hersher, Rebecca. 2018. "Hurricanes Are Moving More Slowly, Which Means More Damage." *All Things Considered (NPR)*, June 6.

Hilfinger Messias, DeAnne K., Clare Barrington, and Elaine Lacy. 2012. "Latino Social Network Dynamics and the Hurricane Katrine Disaster." *Disasters* 36:101–21. DOI:10.1111/j.1467-7717.2011.01243.x.

Holthaus, Eric. 2017. "Harvey Is What Climate Change Looks Like." *Politico*, August 28. www.politico.com.

Horne, Jed. 2006. *Breach of Faith: Hurricane Katrina and the Near Death of a Great American City*. New York: Random House.

Horowitz, Andy. 2017. "Don't Repeat the Mistakes of the Katrina Recovery." *New York Times*, September 14. www.nytimes.com.

Houston, J. Brian. 2012. "Public Disaster Mental/Behavioral Health Communication: Intervention across Disaster Phases." *Journal of Emergency Management* 10:283–92. DOI:10.5055/jem.2012.0106.

Houston, J. Brian, Betty Pfefferbaum, and Cathy E. Rosenholtz. 2012. "Disaster News: Framing and Frame Changing in Coverage of Major U.S. Natural Disasters, 2000–2010." *Journalism & Mass Communication Quarterly* 89:606–23. DOI:10.1177/1077699012456022.

Houston, J. Brian, Matthew L. Spialek, Jennifer First, Jordan Stevens, and Nathan L. First. 2017. "Individual Perceptions of Community Resilience Following the 2011 Joplin Tornado." *Journal of Contingencies and Crisis Management* 25:354–63. DOI:10.1111/1468-5973.12171.

Houston, J. Brian, Matthew L. Spialek, Jordan Stevens, Jennifer First, Vicky L. Mieseler, and Betty Pfefferbaum. 2015a. "2011 Joplin, Missouri Tornado Experience, Mental Health Reactions, and Service Utilization: Cross-Sectional Assessments at Approximately 6 Months and 2.5 Years Post-Event." *PLOS Currents: Disasters* 7. DOI:10.1371/currents.dis.18ca227647291525ce3415bec1406aa5.

Houston, J. Brian, Matthew L. Spialek, Joy Cox, Molly M. Greenwood, and Jennifer First. 2015b. "The Centrality of Communication and Media in Fostering Community Resilience: A Framework for Assessment and Intervention." *American Behavioral Scientist* 59:270–83. DOI:10.1177/0002764214548563.

Jacob, Jeffrey, Merlin Brinkerhoff, Emily Jovic, and Gerald Wheatley. 2004. "The Social and Cultural Capital of Community Currency: An Ithaca HOURS Case Study Survey." *International Journal of Community Currency Research* 8:42–56.

Jang, Sun, Byron R. Johnson, and Young Kim. 2012. "Eagle Scouts: Merit Beyond the Badge." *Faculty Publications—Department of World Languages, Sociology, & Cultural Studies* 39. https://digitalcommons.georgefox.edu/lang_fac/39.

Jokinen-Gordon, Hanna. 2013. "Neighborhoods and Health." Pp. 5–32 in *Poverty and Health*, Vol. 2, *The Importance of Place in Determining Their Future*, edited by K. Fitzpatrick. Santa Barbara, CA: Praeger.

Jones-DeWeever, Avis A., and Heidi Hartmann. 2006. "Abandoned Before the Storms: The Glaring Disaster of Gender, Race, and Class Disparities in the Gulf." Pp. 85–102 in *There is No Such Thing as a Natural Disaster: Race, Class, and Hurricane Katrina*, edited by C. Hartman and G. D. Squires. New York: Routledge.

Joyce, Christopher. 2018. "Record Heat in the Gulf Fueled Hurricane Harvey's Deluge." *NPR*, May 10.

Juan, Angel San. 2018. "Port Arthur's Population Drops by 5,000 after Tropical Storm Harvey." *KFDM*, March 27.

Kaiser Family Foundation. 2017. *An Early Assessment of Hurricane Harvey's Impact on Vulnerable Texans in the Gulf Coast Region: Their Voices and Priorities to Inform Rebuilding Efforts*. Washington, DC: Kaiser Family Foundation.

Kaiser Family Foundation. 2018. *One Year After the Storm: Texas Gulf Coast Residents' Views and Experiences with Hurricane Harvey Recovery. The Kaiser Family Foundation/Episcopal Health Foundation Harvey Anniversary Survey*. Washington, DC: Kaiser Family Foundation.

Kasperson, Roger E., Ortwin Renn, Paul Slovic, Halina Brown, Jacque Emel, Robert Goble, and Samuel Ratick. 1988. "The Social Amplification of Risk: A Conceptual Framework." *Risk Analysis* 8:177–87.

Kawachi, Ichiro, and Lisa F. Berkman. 2003. *Neighborhoods and Health*. New York: Oxford University Press. DOI:10.1093/acprof:oso/9780195138382.001.0001.

Kawachi, Ichiro, S. V. Subramanian, and Daniel Kim. 2008. *Social Capital and Health*. New York: Springer. DOI:10.1007/978-0-387-71311-3_1.

Kim, Yong-Chan, and Jinae Kang. 2010. "Communication, Neighborhood Belonging and Household Hurricane Preparedness." *Disasters* 34:470–88. DOI:10.1111/j.0361-3666.2009.01138.

Kuehnert, Paul. 2018. "Community Resilience in the Eye of a Storm." *Robert Wood Johnson Foundation*. www.rwjf.org.

Kweit, Mary G., and Robert W. Kweit. 2004. "Citizen Participation and Citizen Evaluation in Disaster Recovery." *American Review of Public Administration* 34:354–73.

Lai, Chih-Hui. 2019. "Dormant Disaster Organizing and the Role of Social Media." Pp. 209–25 in *New Media in Times of Crisis*, edited by K. Stephens. New York: Routledge.

Lardieri, Alexa. 2017. "Hurricane Harvey Victims Still Struggling Several Months Later." *US News and World Report*, December 18. www.usnews.com.

Lasker, Judith, Ed Collom, Tara Bealer, Erin Niclaus, Jessica Young Keefe, Zane Kratzer, Lauren Baldasari et al. 2011. "Time Banking and Health: The Role of a Community Currency Organization in Enhancing Well-Being." *Health Promotion Practice* 12:102–15. DOI:10.1177/1524839909353022.

Littlefield, R., Katherine Rowan, Shari R. Veil, Lorraine Kisselburgh, Kimberly Beauchamp, Kathleen Vidoloff, Marie L. Dick et al. 2010. "We Tell People, It's Up to Them to Be Prepared: Public Relations Practices of Local Emergency Managers." Pp. 245–60 in *Handbook of Crisis Communication*, edited by W. T. Coombs and S. J. Holladay. New York: Wiley-Blackwell.

Liu, Brooke F. 2009. "An Analysis of U.S. Government and Media Disaster Frames." *Journal of Communication Management* 13:268–83. DOI:10.1108/13632540910976707.

Liu, Brooke F., Holly Roberts, Elizabeth L. Petrun Sayers, Gray Ackerman, Daniel Smith, and Irina Iles. 2017. "Preparing for the Worst: Public Perceptions of Risk Management Innovations." *Journal of Risk Research* 20:1394–417.

Livingston, Abby. 2019. "U.S. Senate Passes Disaster Aid Bill That Would Release Billions for Harvey Housing Aid." *Texas Tribune*, May 23. https://texastribune.org.

Lozano, Juan. 2018. "Houston Mayor: Recovery From Harvey Not Fast Enough." *US News and World Report*, February 23. www.usnews.com.

Maas, Jimmy. 2017. "High School Football Team Helps Texas Town Rebound After Hurricane Harvey." *All Things Considered (NPR)*, December 23.

Mann, Michael E., Stefan Rahmstorf, Kai Kornhuber, Byron A. Steinman, Sonya K. Miller, and Dim Coumou. 2017. "Influence of Anthropogenic Climate Change on Planetary Wave Resonance and Extreme Weather Events." *Nature Scientific Reports* 7.

Manyena, Bernard, Geoff O'Brien, Phil O'Keefe, and Joanne Rose. 2011. "Disaster Resilience: A Bounce Back or Bounce Forward Ability?" *Local Environment: The International Journal of Justice and Sustainability* 16:417–24.

Massey, Douglas, and Nancy A. Denton. 1993. *American Apartheid: Segregation and the Making of the Underclass.* Cambridge, MA: Harvard University Press.

McFarlane, Alexander C., and Fran H. Norris. 2006. "Definitions and Concepts in Disaster Research." Pp. 3–19 in *Methods for Disaster Mental Health Research*, edited by F. H. Norris, S. Galea, M. J. Friedman, and P. J. Watson. New York: Guilford Press.

Miao, Qing. 2018. "The Fiscal Implications for Managing Natural Disasters for National and Subnational Governments." *Oxford Research Encyclopedia of Natural Hazard Science* 1–38. DOI:10.1093/acrefore/9780199389407.013.194.

Molotch, Harvey, William Freudenberg, and Krista E. Paulsen. 2000. "History Repeats Itself, But How? City Character, Urban Tradition, and the Accomplishment of Place." *American Sociological Review* 65:791–823.

Mouw, Ted. 2006. "Estimating the Causal Effects of Social Capital: A Review of Recent Research." *Annual Review of Sociology* 32:79–102.

Mulilis, John-Paul, and T. Shelley Duval. 1997. "The PrE Model of Coping and Tornado Preparedness: Moderating Effects of Responsibility." *Journal of Applied Social Psychology* 27:1750–66.

National Academies of Science, Engineering, and Medicine. 2019. *Building and Measuring Community Resilience: Actions for Communities and the Gulf Research Program.* Washington, DC: National Academies Press. DOI:10.17226/25383.

National Research Council. 2014. *Reducing Coastal Risk on the East and Gulf Coasts.* Washington, DC: National Academies Press. DOI: 10.17226/18811.

NCEI (National Centers for Environmental Information). 2019. *Billion-Dollar Weather and Climate Disasters: Table of Events.* www.ncdc.noaa.gov.

Neria, Y., A. Nandi, and S. Galea. 2008. "Post-Traumatic Stress Disorder following Disasters: A Systematic Review." *Psychological Medicine* 38:467–80. DOI:10.1017/S0033291707001353.

Nicholls, Susan. 2012. "The Resilient Community and Communication Practice." *Australian Journal of Emergency Management* 27:46–51.

Norris, Fran H., Susan P. Stevens, Betty Pfefferbaum, Karen F. Wyche, and Rose L. Pfefferbaum. 2008. "Community Resilience as a Metaphor, Theory, Set of Capacities, and Strategy for Disaster Readiness." *American Journal of Community Psychology* 41:127–50. DOI:10.1007/s10464-007-9156-6.

Olsen, Lise. 2018. "Record Reservoir Flooding Was Predicted Even Before Harvey Hit Houston." *Houston Chronicle*, February 21. www.houstonchronicle.com.

Padgett, Donyale Renaye. 2002. "Social Work Research on Disasters in the Aftermath of the September 11th Tragedy: Reflections from New York City." *Social Work Research* 26:185–92.

Passel, Jeffrey S., and D'Vera Cohn. 2017. *20 Metro Areas Are Home to Six-in-Ten Unauthorized Immigrants in the U.S.* www.pewresearch.org.

Peacock, Walter, and Chris Girard. 2000. "Ethnic and Racial Inequalities in Hurricane Damage and Insurance Settlements." Pp. 171–90 in *Hurricane Andrew: Ethnicity, Gender, and the Sociology of Disasters*, edited by W. G. Peacock, B. H. Marrow, and H. Gladwin. Miami, FL: International Hurricane Center.

Peacock, Walter G., Betty H. Morrow, and Hugh Gladwin. 1997. *Hurricane Andrew: Ethnicity, Gender and the Sociology of Disasters*. New York: Routledge.

Perry, Ronald W., and Alvin H. Mushkatel. 1986. *Minority Citizen in Disasters*. Athens: University of Georgia Press.

Pfefferbaum, Rose L., Betty Pfefferbaum, and Richard L. Van Horn. 2011. *Communities Advancing Resilience Toolkit (CART): The CART Integrated System*. Oklahoma City: Terrorism and Disaster Center at the University of Oklahoma Health Sciences Center.

Pfefferbaum, Rose L., Betty Pfefferbaum, Pascal Nitiema, J. Brian Houston, and Richard L. Van Horn. 2015. "Assessing Community Resilience: An Application of the Expanded CART Survey Instrument with Affiliated Volunteer Responders." *American Behavioral Scientist* 59:181–99. DOI:10.177/0002764214550295.

Putnam, Robert D. 1995. "Tuning In, Tuning Out: The Strange Disappearance of Social Capital in America." *PS: Political Science and Politics* 28:664–83. DOI:10.2307/420517.

Putnam, Robert D. 2000. *Bowling Alone*. New York: Simon & Schuster.

Putnam, Robert, and Lewis Feldstein. 2003. *Better Together: Restoring the American Community*. New York: Simon & Schuster.

Richardson, Roslyn C., Carol Ann Plummer, Juan J. Barthelemy, and Daphne S. Cain. 2012. "Research after Natural Disasters: Recommendations and Lessons Learned." *Journal of Community Engagement and Scholarship* 2:3–11.

Rivlin, Gary. 2015. *Katrina: After the Flood*. New York: Simon & Schuster.

Ronan, Kevin R., and David M. Johnston. 2003. "Hazards Education for Youth: A Quasi-Experimental Investigation." *Risk Analysis* 23:1009–20. DOI:10.1111/1539-6924.00377.

Ronan, Kevin R., Kylie Crellin, and David M. Johnston. 2010. "Correlates of Hazards Education for Youth: A Replication Study." *Natural Hazards* 53:503–26. DOI:10.1007/s11069-009-9444-6I.

Rosaria, Indah. 2018. "Probing Problems: Dilemmas of Conducting an Ethnographic Study in a Disaster-Affected Area." *International Journal of Disaster Risk Reduction* 31:799–805.

Rosellini, Anthony J., Scott F. Coffey, Melissa Tracy, and Sandro Galea. 2014. "A Person-Centered Analysis of Posttraumatic Stress Disorder Symptoms Following a Natural Disaster: Predictors of Latent Class Membership." *Journal of Anxiety Disorders* 28:16–24. DOI:10.1016/j.janxdis.2013.11.002.

Ross, Ashley, and Lauren A. Clay. 2018. "Capital Assets and Rural Resilience: An Analysis of Texas Communities Impacted by Hurricane Harvey." *Journal of Natural Resources Policy Research* 8:154–84.

Sallis, James F., Neville Owen, and E. B. Fisher. 2008. "Ecological Models of Health Behavior." Pp. 465–85 in *Health Behavior and Health Education: Theory, Research, and Practice*, edited by K. Glanz, B. K. Rimer, and K. Viswanath. San Francisco, CA: Jossey-Bass.

Samenow, Jason. 2017. "60 Inches of Rain Fell from Hurricane Harvey in Texas, Shattering U.S. Storm Record." *Washington Post*, September 22. www.washingtonpost.com.

Sampson, Robert J. 2012. *Great American City: Chicago and the Enduring Neighborhood Effect*. Chicago: University of Chicago Press.

Schmidt, Arjen, Jeroen Wolbers, Julie Ferguson, and Kees Boersma. 2018. "Are You Ready2Help? Conceptualizing the Management of Online and Onsite Volunteer Convergence." *Journal of Contingencies and Crisis Management* 26:338–49. DOI:10.1111/1468-5973.122200.

Schwartz, Rebecca M., Stephanie Tuminello, Samantha M. Kerath, Janelle Rios, Wil Lieberman-Cribbin, and Emanuela Taioli. 2018. "Preliminary Assessment of Hurricane Harvey Exposures and Mental Health Impact." *International Journal of Environmental Research and Public Health* 15:974. DOI:10.3390/ijerph15050974.

Spence, A., W. Poortinga, C. Butler, and N. F. Pidgeon. 2011. "Perceptions of Climate Change and Willingness to Save Energy Related to Flood Experience." *Nature Climate Change* 1:46–49. DOI:10.1038/NCLIMATE1059.

Spence, Patric R., Kenneth A. Lachlan, and Donyale R. Griffin. 2007. "Crisis Communication, Race, and Natural Disasters." *Journal of Black Studies* 37:539–54. DOI:10.1177/0021934706296192.

Spialek, Matthew L., and J. Brian Houston. 2018. "The Development and Initial Validation of the Citizen Disaster Communication Assessment (CDCA)." *Communication Research* 45:934–55. DOI:10.1177/0093650217697521.

Spialek, Matthew L., and J. Brian Houston. 2019. "The Influence of Citizen Disaster Communication on Perceptions of Neighborhood Belonging and Community Resilience." *Journal of Applied Communication Research* 47:1–23. DOI:10.1080/00909882.2018.1544718.

Spialek, Matthew L., J. Brian Houston, and Kyle C. Worley. 2019. "Disaster Communication, Posttraumatic Stress, and Posttraumatic Growth Following Hurricane Matthew." *Journal of Health Communication* 24:65–74. DOI:10.1080/10810730.2019.1574319.

Spittal, Matthew J., John McClure, Richard J. Siegert, and Frank H. Walkey. 2008. "Predictors of Two Types of Earthquake Preparation Activities and Mitigation Activities." *Environment and Behavior* 40:798–817. DOI:10.1177/0013916507309864.

Swartz, Mimi. 2018. "What Houston Didn't Learn from Harvey." *New York Times*, August 24. www.nytimes.com.

Szerter, S., and M. Woolcock. 2004. "Health by Association? Social Capital, Social Theory, and the Political Economy of Public Health." *International Journal of Epidemiology* 33:650–67.

Talarico, Lauren. 2018. "Car Insurance Rates Increase After Harvey." *KHOU11*, March 2.

Tedeschi, Richard G., and Lawrence G. Calhoun. 1996. "The Posttraumatic Growth Inventory: Measuring the Positive Legacy of Trauma." *Journal of Traumatic Stress* 9:455–71. DOI:10.1002/jts.2490090305.

Tedeschi, Richard G., and Lawrence G. Calhoun. 2004. "Posttraumatic Growth: Conceptual Foundations and Empirical Evidence." *Psychological Inquiry* 15:1–18. DOI:10.1207/s15327965pli1501_01.

Theodore, Nik. 2017. *After the Storm: Houston's Day Labor Markets in the Aftermath of Hurricane Harvey*. Great Cities Institute, University of Illinois-Chicago. https://greatcities.uic.edu.

Tierney, Kathleen. 2014. *The Social Roots of Risk: Producing Disasters, Promoting Resilience*. Stanford, CA: Stanford University Press.

Turner, Barry A. 1976. "The Development of Disasters—A Sequence Model for the Analysis of the Origins of Disasters." *Sociological Review* 24:753–74.

Van Zandt, Shannon, Walter Gillis Peacock, Dustin W. Henry, Himanshu Grover, Wesley E. Highfield, and Samuel D. Brody. 2012. "Mapping Social Vulnerability to Enhance Housing and Neighborhood Resilience." *Housing Policy Debate* 22:29–55. DOI:10.1080/10511482.2011.624528.

Wang, Caroline, and Mary Ann Burris. 1997. "Photovoice: Concept, Methodology, and Use for Participatory Needs Assessment." *Health Education & Behavior* 24:369–87.

Washington Post, Kaiser Family Foundation, Harvard School of Public Health. 2005. *Survey of Hurricane Katrina Evacuees*. www.kff.org.

Weiss, D. S. 2007. "The Impact of Event Scale-Revised." Pp. 168–89 in *Assessing Psychological Trauma and PTSD: A Practitioner's Handbook*, edited by J. P. Wilson and T. M. Keane. New York: Guilford Press.

Willis, Adam. 2019. "After Delay Initiated by U.S. Rep Chip Roy, Congress Finally Passes $19.1 Billion Disaster Aid Package." *Texas Tribune*, June 3. https://texastribune.org.

Wilson, Scott. 2018. "Fresh from Hurricane Harvey's Flooding, Houston Starts to Build Anew in the Flood Plain." *Washington Post*, May 22. www.washingtonpost.com.

Witte, Kim. 1992. "Putting the Fear Back into Fear Appeals: The Extended Parallel Process Model." *Communication Monographs* 59:329–49. DOI:10.1080/03637759209376276.

INDEX

Aldrich, Daniel. See *Building Resilience: Social Capital in Post-Disaster Recovery*
American Red Cross, 2
    absence from critical areas, 58–60
    communication difficulties with, 37, 38–39
    disappointing treatment, 65, 67–69
    potential for building community resilience, 153–154
    problems with organization 4, 65
    and shelter experience, 51–53, 95–96, 112
Austin Disaster Relief Network (ADRN), 102–105, 124, 129
    as ecological hub, 102, 128

boat rescues, 48, 90–91, 98, 135, 141
    "Cajun Navy," 3, 47
    community organized, 66
    Hurricane Katrina and, 47
Building Resilience: Social Capital in Post-Disaster Recovery (Aldrich), 40
Bush, President George W., 106

Children's Environmental Health Initiative (CEHI), 120
churches and shelters, 107
    as providers of supplies and support, 65, 100–101
    and utility of faith, 94, 101
CityLab (media outlet), 121–122, 162
    clean up process
        challenges of heavy damage, 58
        damage to possessions, 33, 135

    psychological distress related, 124–125
    climate change, 19-20, 134–135
Communities Advancing Resilience Toolkit, 148
community
    and citizen disaster communication, 165–166
    cleaning help from, 146
    cohesion, 67, 69–73, 81
    connection, 74–78, 98
    connection, lack of, 78
    disaster management, 11, 166
    DNA and, 72–73, 108, 142
    integration, level of, 76
    and planning, 150–151
    and post-Harvey connections, 134, 156
    and preparedness, lack of, 85
    and social capital, role of, 109–112, 141–146
    and support, lack of, 112

Deferred Action for Childhood Arrivals (DACA), 79
disaster management, 108, 141
    Disaster Mitigation Act (2000), 86–87
    disaster planning, 144, 152, 163
disaster mental health
    the bright side of recovery, 130–133
    citizen disaster communication, 143–44
    range of response, 120–124, 127
    role of social support, 73, 134

disinterest. See *New York Times* column
displacement, 9, 50, 117, 121, 127, 165
    climate change and, 133–136
    feelings after, 95
    physical health and, 117

ecological hub, 102. *See also* Austin Disaster Relief Network
ecological microdisaster, as fallout, 18
Environmental Defense Fund, 119
Episcopal Health Foundation, 40. *See also* Kaiser Family Foundation
    Federal Emergency Management Agency (FEMA), 2, 107
    assistance of, 107
    award and application system, 67–68
    charges of incompetence, 107–110
    community DNA concept, 72
        damage estimates, 30–31, 53
    economic infrastructure and, 16–17
    hotel vouchers and, 31, 95
        issues with, 59, 106–108, 130
    Special Flood Hazard Areas designated by, 86–89
    Whole Community approach, 72, 157

financial struggle, 54, 109
finding a place to sleep, 97
    reluctance enter shelters, 96
    PTSD and, 121
flood insurance, 86–88, 157
flood zone, 34, 88–89
food deserts, 6
food insecurity, 121–122

Hurricane Harvey
    anniversary, 115
    early aftermath, 115
    Hurricane Harvey Registry, 128–129
homeowners and renters, 43
hope, 5
Houston
    compared to New Orleans, 10–11

destruction of natural habitat in, 18
    as example of threat from climate change, 20
"Health Villages," 146
police, in shelter, 37
Houston Area Urban League, 125, 155
Houston Chronicle, 83, 115
Houston Community College Warehouse Shelter, 37, 53
Houston Department of Emergency Management, 146
Houston Health Department, 119
Houston Immigration and Legal Services Collaborative (HILSC), 84, 145
hurricanes, other
    Irma, 37, 107
    Katrina, 10, 47, 106, 164
    Maria, 4-5, 37, 47, 107
    Matthew, 144
    Sandy, 160

Kaiser Family Foundation, on Federal role in recovery, 40–42
    assessment at three months, 110
    anniversary survey, 156

National Centers for Environmental Information (NCEI), 19–20
National Flood Insurance Program (NFIP), 86–87
National Science Foundation (NSF), 1, 7, 26, 167
natural disasters, 13–14, 40
New Orleans, 10, 13, 40; Hurricane Katrina, 10, 47, 106, 164
New York Times column (Swarz), 115–116
Northwest Assistance Ministries, 129

Pearland community, 36–37
Photo Voice, 149–150
physical health, 128–130
    of the sheltered vs. not sheltered, 129–130

place, evaluating role of, 3, 8-10, 10–12
   historic patterns of segregation, 10–12
   news coverage limited, 115
   values of, in disaster, 153
Port Arthur, 17–18, 54, 104–105
   population loss, 17
post-trauma social growth, 131–134
preparedness, 7, 11, 73–74, 136, 143, 152
   climate change and, 135–136
   economic status influence, 137
   future, 68–69
   lack of communication about, 82–83, 85
   sustaining resilience 145
   ways to encourage, 152–153, 156
Puerto Rico, 4–7, 47, 166

race/racial, 11, 78, 101, 145, 150
   institutional, 56, 67, 119
   trust, as a crack in resilience, 77–81
   and levels of PTSD, 120–123
   segregation, 10, 12
   struggles, 117, 119, 121
rebuilding, 4, 55–60
   community resilience and, 148
   complications of, 162-164
   social and physical circumstances related to, 160–161
recovery, assessed, 109–111
   coping, 94, 98
   Pearland community response, 37
   positive, 131
   process, 1–4, 41, 147, 157, 160–161
   segregation and, 6–7
   slow, 5, 46, 71, 114, 140, 156
reservoirs, 35, 83
resilience, 4–5, 77, 143–145, 150, 159
   before the storm, 71–72
   recovery and, 7
   risk perception and, 84–89
   social structure and, 10–12
   social trust and, 77–81
   strategies to bolster, 156
   Communities Advancing Resilience Toolkit, 148
   Diverse Disaster Coalition, 150–151
   Emergent Volunteer Groups, 151–152
   when it cracks, 72–74, 103
R. H. Gurwitch Building Community Resilience for Children and Families, 100
Rice University, 119
risk, 75, 85
   perception of, 134, 136
Robert Wood Johnson Foundation, 139, 146
rumors and misinformation, 83
   citizen communication to prevent, 143
   communication failure, 81-82, 144–145
   about FEMA assistance, 109
   about immigrants, 80–81

Salvation Army, 2, 33, 50-51, 58–59, 96
social capital
   bonding, 41, 73, 82, 93, 99, 103, 108–109, 114, 137–138, 155, 158
   bridging, 41, 73, 77–78, 99, 102, 103, 150, 148, 158
   linking, 41, 73, 82, 84, 99, 114, 138, 150–151, 158
   translocal, 102, 103, 105, 145, 148, 156
social media
   Nextdoor app, 153
   rebuilding, 66, 147, 155
social support
   community level, 63, 66
   of friends and family, 50
   of neighbors, 35, 59, 63–64, 98–99
   networks, 6
sociodemographic profile of interviewees, 44-45
socioeconomic status, 99, 118, 131, 149–150
Spanish-language barrier, 83–84, 136, 138, 149–150

support organizations
    Community Self Scale assessment, 77
    local involvement valued, 76–77, 83
    responses viewed as inadequate, 67–69
survey of undocumented immigrants, 80
Swartz, Mimi. See *New York Times* column

temporary shelter, complaints regarding, 51–52
time banks, 154–157; Houston Hours, 156

Trump, President Donald, 80, 105–106, 140–141

US Army Corps of Engineers, 35, 83, 137

volunteers, 3-4, 64, 81, 100, 104–105, 126, 129, 153–154

White House, 5, 105–106, 140
Whole Community disaster management (federal strategy)
    begun under Obama administration, 11–12, 72, 108, 138, 140–142, 157

ABOUT THE AUTHORS

Kevin M. Fitzpatrick, PhD, is a community sociologist with thirty-five years of experience as a researcher, consultant, and advocate. He is a University Professor in the Department of Sociology and Criminal Justice at the University of Arkansas. Since 2005, Kevin has devoted the majority of his work-focus to helping communities throughout Arkansas better understand the challenges they face and the types of strategies they might consider adopting to address those challenges. He has published five books and more than eighty peer-reviewed articles and book chapters that have continually emphasized the theme that *place matters*.

Matthew L. Spialek, PhD, is a disaster communication researcher. He is an Assistant Professor in the Department of Communication at the University of Arkansas. Matthew's research explores how individuals build relationships with organizations and local media in order to foster the civic vitality, public health, and resilience of communities that have experienced or are at risk of experiencing crises and disasters. Matthew has published a number of articles that consistently examine the role of resilience in the natural disaster framework. His most recent work, published in *Communication Research*, *Journal of Applied Communication Research*, and *Journal of Health Communication*, examines the importance of communication systems in helping citizens prepare for, respond to, and recover from natural disasters.

www.ingramcontent.com/pod-product-compliance
Lightning Source LLC
Chambersburg PA
CBHW020254030426
42336CB00010B/756